I0126745

Numismatic and Antiquarian Society of Philadelphia

Proceedings of the Numismatic and Antiquarian Society of

Philadelphia for the Years 1890-1891

Numismatic and Antiquarian Society of Philadelphia

Proceedings of the Numismatic and Antiquarian Society of Philadelphia for the Years 1890-1891

ISBN/EAN: 9783741173127

Manufactured in Europe, USA, Canada, Australia, Japa

Cover: Foto ©Thomas Meinert / pixelio.de

Manufactured and distributed by brebook publishing software
(www.brebook.com)

Numismatic and Antiquarian Society of Philadelphia

Proceedings of the Numismatic and Antiquarian Society of Philadelphia for the Years 1890-1891

Nu:mi's:matic and Antiquarian Society

OF PHILADELPHIA

FOR THE YEARS 1890-1891

PHILADELPHIA

PUBLISHED BY THE SOCIETY

1892

Franklin Printing Company
PHILADELPHIA

CONTENTS.

THE NUMISMATIC AND ANTIQUARIAN SOCIETY OF PHILADELPHIA.

FOUNDED JANUARY 1, 1858.

1890.

OFFICERS.

PRESIDENT.
DANIEL G. BRINTON, M. D.

VICE-PRESIDENTS.

EDWIN W. LEHMAN,
JOHN R. BAKER,
W. S. W. RUSCHENBERGER.

J. SERGEANT PRICE,
REV. JOSEPH F. GARRISON,
LEWIS A. SCOTT,
FRANCIS JORDAN, JR.

HONORARY VICE-PRESIDENTS.

MASSACHUSETTS,	. . . . HON. ROBERT C. WINTHROP,	. . . . . Of Boston.
RHODE ISLAND,	. . . . . . HON. AMOS PERRY, ...	" Providence.
CONNECTICUT,	. . . . HON. J. HAMMOND TRUMBULL, ...	" Hartford.
NEW YORK,	. . . . FREDERIC J. DE PEYSTER, LL. M., . . .	" New York.
DELAWARE,	. . . . . . HON. THOMAS F. BAYARD, ...	" Wilmington.
MARYLAND,	. . . . HON. JOHN H. B. LATROBE, ...	" Baltimore.
DISTRICT OF COLUMBIA,	. DR. G. BROWN GOODE, ...	" Washington.
VIRGINIA,	. . . . R. ALONZO BROCK, ESQ., ...	" Richmond.
GEORGIA,	. . . . CHARLES C. JONES, JR., ESQ., ...	" Augusta.
LOUISIANA,	. . . . . JOSEPH JONES, M. D., ...	" New Orleans.
WISCONSIN,	. . . . . . PROF. JAMES D. BUTLER, ...	" Madison.
IOWA,	. . . . RT. REV. WILLIAM STEVENS PERRY, .	" Davenport.
CALIFORNIA,	. . . . . . RT. REV. WILLIAM INGRAHAM KIP, . .	" San Francisco.

Corresponding Secretary, . . . HENRY PHILLIPS, JR.
Recording Secretary, ... STEWART CULIN.
Treasurer, ... THOMAS HOCKLEY.
Historiographer, ... FRANK WILLING LEACH.
Curator of Numismatics, . . . FREDERICK D. LANGENHEIM.
Curator of Antiquities, . . . CORNELIUS STEVENSON.
Librarian, ... INMAN HORNER.

COMMITTEES.

COMMITTEE ON NUMISMATICS.
FREDERICK D. LANGENHEIM,
WILLIAM S. BAKER,
GEORGE PEIRCE.

COMMITTEE ON GENEALOGY.
JOSEPH H. COATES,
CHARLES HENRY HART,
FRANK WILLING LEACH.

COMMITTEE ON LIBRARY.
HENRY C. LEA,
JOHN M. SCOTT,
REV. JOSEPH F. GARRISON.

COMMITTEE ON ANTIQUITIES.
FRANCIS JORDAN, JR.,
WESTCOTT BAILEY,
BENJAMIN SMITH LYMAN.

COMMITTEE ON FINANCE.
J. SERGEANT PRICE,
HENRY IUNGERICH,
WILLIAM LONGSTRETH.

COMMITTEE ON HALL.
THOMAS HOCKLEY,
JOSEPH WRIGHT,
ELI KIRK PRICE.

COMMITTEE ON PUBLICATION.
STEWART CULIN,
EDWIN W. LEHMAN,
BENJAMIN SMITH LYMAN.

Hall of the Society, Northwest Corner Eighteenth and Chestnut Streets.

1891.

OFFICERS.

PRESIDENT.
DANIEL G. BRINTON, M. D..

VICE-PRESIDENTS.

EDWIN W. LEHMAN,	J. SERGEANT PRICE,
JOHN R. BAKER,	REV. JOSEPH F. GARRISON,
W. S. W. RUSCHENBERGER,	LEWIS A. SCOTT,

FRANCIS JORDAN, JR.

HONORARY VICE-PRESIDENTS.

HON. ROBERT C. WINTHROP, ... Massachusetts.
HON. AMOS PERRY, ... Rhode Island.
HON. J. HAMMOND TRUMBULL, ... Connecticut.
FREDERIC J. DE PEYSTER, LL.M., ... New York.
HON. THOMAS F. BAYARD, ... Delaware.
HON. JOHN H. B. LATROBE, ... Maryland.
PROF. G. BROWN GOODE, ... District of Columbia.
R. ALONZO BROCK, ESQ., ... Virginia.
CHARLES C. JONES, JR., ESQ., ... Georgia.
JOSEPH JONES, M. D., ... Louisiana.
PROF. JAMES D. BUTLER, ... Wisconsin.
RT. REV. WILLIAM STEVENS PERRY, ... Iowa.
RT. REV. WILLIAM INGRAHAM KIP, ... California.

Corresponding Secretary,	. . . HENRY PHILLIPS, JR.
Recording Secretary,	. . . . . STEWART CULIN.
Treasurer,	. . . . THOMAS HOCKLEY.
Historiographer,	. . . . ELI KIRK PRICE.
Curator of Numismatics,	. . . FREDERICK D. LANGENHEIM.
Curator of Antiquities,	. . . . CARL EDELHEIM.
Librarian,	. . . . INMAN HORNER.

COMMITTEES.

COMMITTEE ON NUMISMATICS.
FREDERICK D. LANGENHEIM,
J. COLVIN RANDALL,
HARRY ROGERS.

COMMITTEE ON GENEALOGY.
JOSEPH H. COATES,
G. ALBERT LEWIS,
ELI K. PRICE,

COMMITTEE ON LIBRARY.
JOHN M. SCOTT,
DAVID MILNE,
CARL EDELHEIM.

COMMITTEE ON ANTIQUITIES.
CLARENCE S. BEMENT,
BENJAMIN SMITH LYMAN,
MAXWELL SOMMERVILLE.

COMMITTEE ON FINANCE.
J. SERGEANT PRICE,
HENRY IUNGERICH,
WILLIAM LONGSTRETH.

COMMITTEE ON HALL.
THOMAS HOCKLEY,
B. V. MEIN,
FRANCIS JORDAN, JR.

COMMITTEE ON PUBLICATION.
STEWART CULIN,   REV JOSEPH F. GARRISON,
BENJAMIN SMITH LYMAN.

Hall of the Society, Southeast Corner Twenty-first and Pine Streets.

Abbott, Harry J., 1509 Locust Street, Philadelphia.

Anderson, Joseph W., M. D., Ardmore, Pa.

Bailey, Westcott, 1020 Chestnut Street, Philadelphia.

Bailey, B. N., 2115 Spruce Street, Philadelphia.

Baird, John, 1705 North Broad Street, Philadelphia.

*Baker, Alfred G., 421 Walnut Street, Philadelphia.

Baugh, Samuel, 2025 Chestnut Street, Philadelphia.

Bement, Clarence S., 1804 Spring Garden Street, Philadelphia.

Brinton, Daniel G., M. D., 2041 Chestnut Street, Philadelphia.

Brock, R. C. H., 222 South Nineteenth Street, Philadelphia.

Clark, Charles D., 2215 Spruce Street, Philadelphia.

Clark, Clarence H., 4116 Spruce Street, Philadelphia.

Coates, Joseph H., 116 Chestnut Street, Philadelphia.

*Cramp, Henry W., 1736 Spring Garden Street, Philadelphia.

Culin, Stewart, University of Pennsylvania.

Dana, Charles E., 2013 DeLancey Pl., Philadelphia.

Davis, Robert S., 1801 Spruce Street, Philadelphia.

Disston, Hamilton, Bullitt Building, Philadelphia.

Dolan, Thomas, 1809 Walnut Street, Philadelphia.

Donaldson, Thomas, 326 North Thirty-ninth Street, Philadelphia.

Drexel, Anthony J., Thirty-ninth and Walnut Streets, Philadelphia.

Edelheim, Carl, 202 West Logan Square, Philadelphia.

Eyre, Wilson, 927 Chestnut Street, Philadelphia.

Fitler, Edwin H., 1600 Walnut Street, Philadelphia.

Flanigen, William A., 2120 Spruce Street, Philadelphia.

Garrett, P. C., Logan Station, Philadelphia.

Gutekunst, Frederick, 712 Arch Street, Philadelphia.

Harrison, Charles C., 1618 Locust Street, Philadelphia.

*Hart, Charles Henry, Drexel Building, Philadelphia.

Horner, Inman, Rittenhouse Club, Philadelphia.

*Hutchinson, Charles H., 1617 Walnut Street, Philadelphia.

Iüngerich, Henry, 1721 Spruce Street, Philadelphia.

Jenks, John Story, 1937 Arch Street, Philadelphia.

Jordan, Francis, Jr., 4107 Spruce Street, Philadelphia.

Lamborn, Dr. Robert H., 32 Nassau Street, New York City.

Langenheim, F. D., Ardmore, Pa.

Lea, Charles M., 2006 Walnut Street, Philadelphia.

Lea, Henry C., 2000 Walnut Street,
Philadelphia.
Leach, Frank Willing, 733 Walnut
Street, Philadelphia.
Lehman, Edwin W., 1718 Arch Street,
Philadelphia.
Lewis, G. Albert, 1834 DeLancey Pl.,
Philadelphia.
Longstreth, William, 2013 Chestnut
Street, Philadelphia.
*Lyman, Benjamin Smith, 708 Locust
Street, Philadelphia.

Mein, B. V., 619 Market Street, Phila-
adelphia.
Milne, Caleb J., 2030 Walnut Street,
Philadelphia.
Milne, David, 2030 Walnut Street,
Philadelphia.
*Moore, Clarence B., cor. Juniper and
Locust Streets, Philadelphia.
Morris, John T., 826 Pine Street, Phila-
delphia.
Moses, Rev. John Robert, 816 Franklin
Street, Philadelphia.
Myer, Isaac, 21 East Sixtieth Street,
New York City.

Newhall, George M., 119 South Fourth
Street, Philadelphia.

Patterson, Joseph Storm, 1511 Spruce
Street, Philadelphia.
Peirce, George, 623 Walnut Street,
Philadelphia.
Pepper, William, M. D., 1811 Spruce
Street, Philadelphia.

Perkins, Samuel C., 627 Walnut Street,
Philadelphia.
Price, Eli Kirk, 709 Walnut Street,
Philadelphia.
Price, J. Sergeant, 709 Walnut Street.
Philadelphia.

Randall, J. Colvin, 1905 Chestnut St.,
Philadelphia.
Ritchie, Craig D., 1001 Chestnut Street.
Philadelphia.
Rogers, Harry, 1822 Spruce Street,
Philadelphia.
Ruschenberger, Dr. W. S. W., 1932
Chestnut Street, Philadelphia.

Scott, John M., 118 South Eighteenth
Street, Philadelphia.
Scott, Lewis A., 1806 Locust Street,
Philadelphia.
Smedley, Samuel L., New City Hall,
Philadelphia.
Sommerville, Maxwell, 311 South Tenth
Street, Philadelphia.
Stevenson, Cornelius, 603 Walnut Street,
Philadelphia.

Todd, M. Hampton, 731 Walnut Street,
Philadelphia.

*Wagner, H. Dumont, 1432 Pine Street,
Philadelphia.
Wiseman, John, 125 South Front Street,
Philadelphia.
Wright, Joseph, 2023 Walnut Street.
Philadelphia.

HONORARY MEMBERS.

Ahlborn, Madame Lea, Stockholm, Sweden.

Bayard, Thomas F., Wilmington, Del.
Butler, James D., Madison, Wis.

Evans, John, Nash Mills, Hemel Hempstead, England.

Jones, Charles C., Jr., Augusta, Ga.
Jones, Joseph, M. D., New Orleans, La.

Kip, Rt. Rev. William Ingram, San Francisco, Cal.

Levasseur, Emil, Paris, France.

Madden, Frederick W., Brighton, Eng.
Muoni, Damiano, Milan, Italy.
Murray, James A. H., London, Eng.

Owen, Sir P. Cunliffe, London, Eng.

Patterson, James W., Hanover, N. H.
Perry, Rt. Rev. William Stevens, Davenport, Iowa.

Winthrop, Robert C., Boston, Mass.

CORRESPONDING MEMBERS.

Abbott, Charles C., M. D., Bristol, N. J.
Adam, Lucien, Rennes, France.
Adams, Herbert B., Baltimore, Md.
Alvarez, Antonio Machaday, Madrid, Spain.
Ambiveri, Luigi, Milan, Italy.
Appleton, William S., Boston, Mass.
Axon, W. E. A., Manchester, Eng.
Aymé, Louis H., Merida, Yucatan.

Bancroft, Hubert Howe, San Francisco, Cal.
Barber, Edwin A., West Chester, Pa.
Beauchamp, W. M., Baldwinsville, N.Y.
Bergsoe, Vilhelm, Copenhagen, Denmark.
Biondelli, B., Milan, Italy.
Blumer, F. Imhoof, Winterthur, Switzerland.
Boaz, Franz, Worcester, Mass.
Bolton, H: Carrington, New York, N. Y.

Bradlee, Rev. Caleb Davis, Boston, Mass.
Broek, Robert Alonzo, Richmond, Va.
Brown, John Marshall, Portland, Me.
Bryant, Hubbard Winslow, Portland, Me.
Bulliott, J. G., Autun, France.
Cannizzaro, Tommaso, Messina, Italy.
Carutti di Cantogna, Baron D., Rome. Italy.
Castellani, Alessandro, Rome, Italy.
Clarke, Robert, Cincinnati, Ohio.
Colburn, Jeremiah, Boston, Mass.
Coleman, Mrs. G. Dawson, Lebanon, Pa.
Comfort, Aaron J., M. D., New Mexico.
Cournault, Charles, Malzeville, France.

De Costa, Rev. B. F., New York, N. Y.
Darling, C. W., Utica, N. Y.

11

Da Silva, J. P. N., Lisbon, Portugal.
Davenport, Henry, Boston, Mass.
Davis, W. W. H., Doylestown, Pa.
Dean, John Ward, Boston, Mass.
Deans, John, Victoria, British Columbia.
De Charency, Comte Hyacinthe, St. Maurice Les Charency, France.
De Cleve, Jules, Mons, Belgium.
Deinvilliers, Leopold, Mons, Belgium.
D'Ernst, Charles, Vienna, Austria.
Del Már, Alexander, San Francisco, Cal.
De Olaguibel, Manuel, Mexico.
De Peyster, J. Watts, Tivoli, N. Y.
De Rochambeau, Marquis A., Paris, France.
De Rosny, Léon, Paris, France.
De Vere, M. Schele, Charlottesville, Va.
Di 'Cesnola, Louis P., New York, N. Y.
Dobroczky, Ignaz, Heves, Hungary.
Dohrn, Charles A., Stettin, Prussia.
Donner, Otto, Helsingfors, Finland.
Dorsey, J. Owen, Washington, D. C.
Drowne, Henry T., New York, N. Y.
Durand, John, Paris, France.
Durrie, Daniel S., Madison, Wis.
Duruy, Victor, Paris, France.

Egle, William H., M. D., Harrisburg, Pa.

Field, Osgood, London, England.
Forscheimer, Edward, Vienna, Austria.

Gatschet, Albert S., Washington, D. C.
Gilman, Daniel C., Baltimore, Md.
Glatz, A. Hiestand, York, Pa.
Green, Samuel A., M. D., Boston, Mass.
Griffin, Rev. George H., Milford, Conn.

Hadi, Syad Mohammed, Sultanpur, India.
Hale, Horatio, Clinton, Ontario, Canada.
Hamy, Dr. E. T., Paris, France.
Haynes, Henry W., Boston, Mass.
Head, Barclay V., London, Eng.
Herbage, William, London, Eng.

Herbst, C. F., Copenhagen, Denmark.
Herndon, William H., Springfield, Ill.
Hildebrand, Bror Emil, Stockholm, Sweden.
Hildebrand, Hans, Stockholm, Sweden.
Hoffman, W. J., M. D., Washington, D. C.
Holmes, George A., Montreal, Canada.
Holmes, Nathaniel, Cambridge, Mass.
Holmes, Oliver Wendell, Boston, Mass.
Horner, Frederick, Jr., M. D., Salem, Va.
Hovelacque, Abel, Paris, France.
Huguet-Latour, Major, Montreal, Canada.

Im Thurn, E. F., Georgetown, British Guiana.

Jenkins, Howard M., Gwynedd, Pa.

Karabacek, Joseph, Vienna, Austria.
Keary, C. F., London, Eng.
Kenner, Friedrich, Vienna, Austria.
Kochler, S. R., Washington, D. C.
Konstostaulas, A., Athens, Greece.
Krause, Prof. W., Göttingen, Germany.
Krauss, Friedrich S., Vienna, Austria.

Leibert, Rev. Eugene, Nazareth, Pa.
Le Moine, J. M., Quebec, Canada.
Lindsley, J. Berrien, M. D., Nashville, Tenn.
Long, Rev. Albert L., Constantinople.
Loring, Charles G., Boston, Mass.
Low, Lyman H., New York, N. Y.
Lubbock, Sir John, London, Eng.

Macauley, Francis C., Florence, Italy.
Macedo, Dr. José, Seville, Spain.
Madrazo, D. Pedro, Madrid, Spain.
Mallery, Garrick, Washington, D. C.
March, Francis A., Easton, Pa.
Marsh, Othniel C., New Haven, Conn.
Marvin, W. T. R., Boston, Mass.
Mercur, Rodney A., Towanda, Pa.
Merzbacher, Eugene, Munich, Germany.
Meyer, C., Hamburg, Germany
Mitchell, Arthur, Edinburgh, Scotland.
Moore, Charles B., New York, N. Y.
Morse, Edward S., Salem, Mass.

Mott, Henry, Montreal, Canada.
Much, M., Vienna, Austria.

Nadaillac, Le Marquis de, Paris, France.
Nicolaysen, N., Christiana, Norway.

Paine, Nathaniel, Worcester, Mass.
Parkman, Francis, Boston, Mass.
Peñafiel, Antonio, Mexico.
Plix, M. J., Amsterdam, Holland.
Poillon, William, New York, N. Y
Poniatowsky, L., St. Petersburg, Russia.
Poole, William F., Chicago, Ill.
Portioli, Attilio, Mantua, Italy.
Post, George E., M. D., Smyrna, Turkey.
Postalacca, Achille, Athens, Greece.
Putnam, Fred. W., Cambridge, Mass.

Ridgway, Rev. James, Oxford, Eng.
Riggauer, Dr. Hans, Munich, Germany.
Robinson, George E., Cardiff, Wales.
Roest, T. M., Leyden, Holland.
Rogers, Rev. Charles, London, Eng.
Rossi, Chevalier, Rome, Italy.

Salisbury, Stephen, Jr., Worcester, Mass.
Sanchez, Jesus, Mexico.
Seletti, Emilio, Milan, Italy.
Sergi, Giuseppe, Rome, Italy.
Serrure, Raymond, Bruxelles, Belgium.
Seymour, Frederick H., Detroit, Mich.
Sharpless, Alfred, West Chester, Pa.

Slafter, Rev. Edmund F., Boston, Mass.
Stevens, John Austin, New York, N. Y.
Stiles, Henry R., M. D., Brooklyn, N. Y.
Strong, Herbert A., Melbourne, Australia.
Sweeny, Robert O., M. D., St. Paul, Minn.
Szombathy, Joseph, Vienna, Austria.

Taine, M. Hippolite, France.
Thomas, Thomas H., Cardiff, Wales.
Thorsteinson, Arni, Reykjavik, Iceland.
Thruston, Gates P., Nashville, Tenn.
Toppan, Robert Noxon, Boston, Mass.
Trask, Wm. Blake, Boston, Mass.
Trau, Franz, Vienna, Austria.
Trumbull, J. Hammond, Hartford, Conn.

Von Meltzel, Hugo, Koloszvar, Hungary.
Von Raiman, Franz, Vienna, Austria.
Von Tiesenhausen, Prof. W., St. Petersburg.
Vors, Frederick, New York, N. Y.

Wheatland, Henry, Salem, Mass.
Williams, J. Fletcher, St. Paul, Minn.
Wilmorsdörffer, Max, Munich.
Wilson, Sir Daniel, Toronto, Canada.
Winks, Rev. William E., Cardiff, Wales.
Winsor, Justin, Cambridge, Mass.
Wood, Isaac F., New York, N. Y.
Wouvermans, Col. Henry, Antwerp, Belgium.

DONORS TO THE LIBRARY 1890-91.

(I) INDIVIDUALS.

Bancroft, Herbert Howe, San Francisco, Cal.

Barber, Edwin A., West Chester, Pa.

Bolton, H. Carrington, New York city.

Bradlee, Rev. C. D., Boston, Mass.

Brinton, Dr. Daniel G., Philadelphia.

Carotti, Cav. Giulio, Milan, Italy.

Carrillo y Ancona, Don Cresencio, Merida, Yucatan.

Conover, George S., Geneva, N. Y.

Culin, Stewart, Philadelphia.

Darling, Gen. C. W., Utica, N. Y.

De Charency, M. le Comte, St. Maurice les Charency. France.

. De Peyster, Maj.-Gen. J. Watts, Tivoli, N. Y.

De Rosny, Léon, Paris, France.

Dorsey, Rev. J. Owen, Washington, D. C.

Gatschet, Albert S., Washington, D. C.

Hale, Horatio, Clinton, Ontario.

Handelmann, H.

Hart, Charles Henry, Philadelphia.

Hockley, Thomas, Philadelphia.

Hovelacque, Abel, Paris, France.

Jones, Col. Charles C., Jr., Augusta, Ga.

Leech, Hon. Edward O., Washington, D. C.

Macauley, Francis C., Florence, Italy.

Mallery, Col. Garrick, Washington, D. C.

Moore, Clarence B., Philadelphia.

Patterson, Joseph Storm, Philadelphia.

Perkins, Samuel C., Philadelphia.

Perry, Hon. Amos, Providence, R. I.

Phillips, Henry, Jr., Philadelphia.

Quaritch, Bernard, London, Eng.

Sambon, Arturo G., Rome, Italy.

Seletti, Emilio, Milan, Italy

Thomas, Thomas H., Cardiff, Wales.

Thruston, G. P., Nashville, Tenn.

Topinard, Paul, Paris, France.

Trübner, Messrs. & Co., London, Eng.

Von Höfken, Rudolph, Vienna.

Winks, Rev. William E., Cardiff, Wales.

(II) SOCIETIES AND INSTITUTIONS.

IN THE UNITED STATES.

University of California, Berkeley, Cal.
Historical Society of Delaware, Wilmington.
Bureau of Ethnology, Washington, D. C.
Bureau of Education, Washington, D. C.
Department of State, Washington, D. C.
Smithsonian Institution, Washington, D. C.
Kansas Academy of Science, Kansas.
Bostonian Society, Boston, Mass.
Museum of Fine Arts, Boston, Mass.
Peabody Museum of American Archaeology and Ethnology, Cambridge, Mass.
Essex Institute, Salem, Mass.
Minnesota Historical Society, St. Paul, Minn.
New Jersey Historical Society, Newark, N. J.
Buffalo Historical Society, Buffalo, N. Y.
American Numismatic and Archaeological Society, New York, N. Y.
Oneida Historical Society, Utica, N. Y.
American Philosophical Society, Philadelphia, Pa.
Department of Archaeology and Palaeontology of the University of Pennsylvania, Philadelphia, Pa.
Library Company of Philadelphia, Philadelphia, Pa.
Wyoming Historical and Geological Society, Wilkesbarre, Pa.
Rhode Island Historical Society, Providence, R. I.
Virginia Historical Society, Richmond, Va.
State Historical Society of Wisconsin, Madison, Wis.

IN FOREIGN COUNTRIES.

Institut Égyptien, Cairo, Egypt.
North China Branch of the Royal Asiatic Society, Shanghai, China.
Bataviaansche Genootschap van Kunsten en Wetenschappen, Batavia, Java.
K. K. Naturhistorisches Hof-Museum, Vienna, Austria.
Numismatische Gesellschaft, Vienna, Austria.
Cercle Archéologique, Mons, Belgium.
Musée Guimet, Paris, France.
Société d' Anthropologie, Paris, France.
Société d' Emulation des Côtes-du-Nord, Saint-Brieuc, France.
Numismatische Gesellschaft, Berlin, Germany.
Alterthums-Verein, München, Germany.
Cambridge Antiquarian Society, Cambridge, England.
Numismatic Society, London, England.
Royal Historical and Archaeological Association of Ireland, Kilkenny, Ireland.
Philosophical Society, Glasgow, Scotland.
R. Accademia di Scienze e Lettere e Belle Arti, Palermo, Italy.
R. Accademia dei Lincei, Rome, Italy.
Société Finno-Ougrienne, Helsingfors, Finland.
Moscow Archaeological Society, Moscow, Russia.
Imperial Russian Archaeological Society, St. Petersburg, Russia.
Kongl. Vitterhets Historie och Antiquitets Akademien, Stockholm, Sweden.

DONORS TO THE CABINET 1890-91.

Chatelain, Héli, Angola, Africa.
Culin, Stewart, Philadelphia.
Jordan, Francis, Jr., Philadelphia.
Macauley, Francis C., Florence, Italy.

Patterson, Joseph Storm, Philadelphia.
Phillips, Henry, Jr., Philadelphia.
Rogers, Harry, Philadelphia.

DONORS OF MONEY,

TO REDUCE THE MORTGAGE ON THE HALL.

Alfred G. Baker,	$25
Samuel Baugh,	100
Charles C. Harrison,	50
Charles Hare Hutchinson,	50
William Longstreth,	100
J. Sergeant Price,	100
Lewis A. Scott,	100
	$525

JANUARY 2D.

President Brinton delivered the annual address, his subject being
" Enigmas in American Archæology."

After referring to the increased attention paid of late years to the
study of the antiquities of America, he said the result of these studies
had been to increase the problems offered by the ancient history of
America. " Right here, in the valley of the Delaware River, remains
had been found assigning man a residence along the river when the
reindeer and the wild peccary were his companions, and when the
great ice sheet covered the whole continent to the north. Recent
explorations in Florida reveal the existence there at no very remote
age of a dense and cultivated population. The examination of
mounds along the Ohio had disclosed a condition of the arts among
the people who built them not unworthy of comparison with the
ancient Greek colonies. In Arizona industrial works had been discovered of vast extent and unknown antiquity ; and in Mexico and
Central America researches are constantly bringing to light new and
surprising remains of the former occupants of the land." The
speaker closed by urging the prime importance of early and extended
research and collection in the field of American archæology.

Mr. Thomas Hockley presented a copy of the beautiful bronze medal
awarded by the Pennsylvania Museum and School of Industrial Art at
the recent exhibition of ceramics in Memorial Hall, Fairmount Park.

The death of the Hon. George H. Boker, a life member of the
Society, was announced as having taken place on the day of the
meeting, in the 67th year of his age.

FEBRUARY 6TH.

Dr. Charles C. Abbott delivered an address entitled " The Prehistoric Coppersmiths of Wisconsin." After referring to the scarcity of
copper implements among the remains found on the Atlantic coast,

although native copper occurs, the speaker stated the central point in the United States for this metal is in the State of Wisconsin, and that here, naturally, the most important discoveries of worked copper have been made. A collection of copper implements from Marquette County, Wisconsin, numbering 560 objects, all found on a small field of about five acres and the result of thirty years' gathering, was then described. This remarkable collection is now in the Museum of Archæology of the University of Pennsylvania. From it a small number of typical objects were exhibited. Among them were four fish-hooks which present a remarkable similarity to the bronze fish-hooks found in the Swiss lake dwellings. A celt, a knife, a spear point with a peculiar haft, an awl pointed at both ends, and a spoon-shaped object, which is really a form of knife peculiar to this country, were also shown. The speaker was positive that none of these objects were molded. Dr. Kœnig, of the University, had examined them, and concurred with Dr. Abbott in his opinion.

In connection with the copper implements a collection of 3,000 objects of stone from the same field was sent. Some of these were stated to be forms not found in other parts of the United States, and apparently modeled on those of the coppers. At the conclusion of Dr. Abbott's remarks, President Brinton referred to the effort that had been made on the part of some archæologists to insert an additional period between the age of stone and the age of bronze; this is the age of copper, and the objects in the present collection afford the strongest confirmation of that view. But they must be regarded, according to Dr. Brinton, simply as malleable stone, and belonging to the stone age. These implements are remarkable for their correspondence with the bronze objects found in Europe. The early workers in metal imitated the forms of the stone implements, and the knife of peculiar form in the present collection was probably copied from the semi-lunar form of the flint knife. The exploitation of copper in the Lake Superior region must be regarded as prehistoric, and the mines had all been abandoned at the time of the first contact with foreigners.

Two copper beads in the Society's collection from Rehoboth, Del., which had been originally obtained at the sale of Long's Museum, were exhibited and their antiquity discussed. Dr. Abbott stated that many such beads were made from brass obtained from the first settlers, brass kettles and afterward sheet brass being eagerly purchased by the Indians for this purpose. The fact that the metal of these beads was brass or native copper would determine their character.

The Rev. Dr. Joseph F. Garrison spoke as follows on

"THE COSMIC ETHER."

The term "antiquarian" is usually applied to the study of things. My remarks have to do with the history of ideas, and I wish to show the curious vitality of certain ideas, which, originally mere metaphysical conceptions resting upon no foundation of fact or experiment, are now coming up again in these later days among the mathematical verities of science.

It is extremely curious that the assumption of a cosmic ether, one of the latest conclusions of modern science, compelled by the severest necessities of mathematics in the two great subjects of astronomy (comets) and of light (the undulatory theory), should have been one of the essential elements of the speculations, theologic and philosophic, of the remote East, and should have reappeared ever since in almost every age, and been a vital element in almost every system of attempts to account for the phenomena of nature, from the Hindu Upanishads to that of the great Berkeley, Bishop of Cloyne. It reappears again in the wholly opposite spheres of thought represented by Clerk Maxwell in *Science* and Elias Levi in *Theosophy*, not to mention the very remarkable attempt of the two distinguished Edinburgh scientists, Professors Stewart and Tait, in their most suggestive book, *The Unseen Universe*, to find in it the origin and continuance of life, and its re-incorporation in new and higher forms after death.

The interesting point in the cosmic ether as a subject of antiquarian study is the fact of the early existence of a belief in some universal substance of an infinitely more refined and subtle nature than any form of matter known to us, and which is either regarded as itself a primitive force and source of action or creation, or the primary medium on which and from which the Supreme Intellect was able to form and keep in action all portions of the universe. The ablest thinkers in most cosmogonies of which we have any knowledge assume as one of their fundamental elements an agent, rendered generally by some word corresponding to our term cosmic ether, which has essentially the same feature as the substance now regarded by the necessities of the highest mathematics as a factor in the calculations of the exact sciences of light and astronomy.

In the Upanishads it has a vitally important place. Its Hindu name is *Akasa*, not a physical ether, but that potential somewhat from which all things come, and which indeed in a sense is ALL. It is identified with light and the manifestations of Brahma and in a sense with space.

When we come to the Greeks, we find that Pherecydes was in possession of a similar idea to that held by the Hindus regarding the primitive elements of the universe. He makes three primal powers or universal substances. Zeus, ether, the active principle in all; Earth, the passive, and Time, that in which Ether and Earth produce all things. Anaximander considered the origin of all things as an aeriform substance, eternal and imperishable, embracing and governing all; in effect, an ether having spontaneous and eternal movement. This incorporeal principle has an eternal activity, and thereby produces a sort of evolution by which it evolves concrete and finite realities. The first forms of these are air and fire. Anaximenes declared that the entire world has for principle of unity, and at the same time principle of life, a universal air; so that the world is a living being, and that this air (evidently the same in property as ether) can scarcely be distinguished from matter, and yet it is that which moves all and produces all—is a substance infinite and invisible—in fact, God Himself. Heraclitus does not employ in this connection "ether," but has a curious pre-intimation of the fact, now scientific, that light, fire, heat, and electricity are all only various forms of the one universal potential substance. He calls it fire. Not fire as we know it, but that subtile fire that causes all things and into which all things return.

If we follow down the whole line of phases under which the philosophers presented parallel ideas, all implying the existence of a universal, exquisitely subtle substance which was itself the form in which cosmic thought existed and evolved the universe, or which was the prime and universal material out of which the cosmic thought evolved all things, we find it was called by several names—fire, the Infinite, air, or more frequently ether, and possessed the marvelous faculty that out of it the primeval elements were all produced. These themselves were regarded as mutually resolvable into one another. Fire could become light—light, fire. Ether might be transformed into life, and some even fancied, in its eventual workings, it was thought;—a most curious foreshadowing in many forms of the modern doctrine of conservation of energy and interchange of the vital or fundamental forces, which first became popularized in Tyndall's book, *Heat, as a Mode of Motion*. Plato and the Stoics assume in various ways the existence of some such substance or mode of action as the essential element of the cosmic universe. In the Phœnician mythology are references to a like universal fundamental agent called sometimes air, alluded to as aeriform and posited as the substance out of which all things were made.

During the period from the last of all classical philosophy and general literature we have no speculations worth noting on this or any other matter not immediately connected with the peculiar phases of Middle Age philosophy and ritual; but among the earliest exhibitions of the renewal of thought we find a reappearance, whether by a rediscovery in the old Greek and Indian writers, or because one of the permanent ideas of the race, it comes to the surface on every occasion. We find it in the Gnostic system; in the Kaballa; in the Occultists; in the Magicians; in so great a modern thinker as Bishop Berkeley; and finally taking its place, not as a metaphysical hypothesis or fancy, but as a bald mathematical necessity.

A conception of the existence of such universal ether with a claim to knowledge how to use and utilize its various forces, is the foundation of all the occult sciences, whether in the refined and subtle Hindu systems of twenty-five hundred years ago, or the new forms of occultism in the Middle Ages and certain of their followers of to-day. Infinite contempt and jest has been and is yet cast upon their claims, but the latest results of Clerk Maxwell and Professors Stewart and Tait must relieve them from much of this. These writers more than hint that there is a world-pervading and a world-active substance, in which the universal forces of heat, light, electricity, motion, and other cosmic forces are essentially inherent; and also that one who knows can transmute heat into light; can, by motion, transmute either of them into electricity, or this into any or all of the others. Many assert, not obscurely, that under fitting circumstances they can evolve life, and that life, again, may be elevated into intellect. In other words, that there is a universal substance which, whether by a potency of its own or that of a Being from without, can be made to take on any of the cosmic forces and can enable them to interchange, moreover, that this one substance is common to all things, and that it may, by one who knows how to employ the force in it, be made into any of them or anything may be transmuted back into this one substance and reproduced in another form—that is, that he who knows how to deal with the force of this ether may not only transmute heat into electricity, but copper into gold; can indeed by the action of these forces obtain the elixir of life. I should be very far from admitting the possibility of any of these latter statements, yet not more so than David Hume would have been from admitting the notion that a baby's touch in Liverpool could be transmitted into an electric current that could convey beneath the ocean the subtle reasoning of his marvelous essays.

We have seen this conception that now plays so large a part in our latest mathematical science make its appearance in the earliest ages of philosophy as one of its most tenacious assumptions. This not in one line, but many: the Hindus; a long line of the Greeks; the later Neo-Alexandrians; the Old Testament; the philosophic Gnostics; the subtle Kaballists; the Occultists of the Middle Ages; the alchemists and magicians; the marvelous system of Paracelsus and Jacob Boehme; the present school of quack mesmerists, and the most careful students of hypnotism. Besides these, one of the most remarkable of all the writings of Bishop Berkeley, *Siris*, is an elaborate and most extraordinary endeavor to show that it was impossible for science to construct a theory of the universe, even in his day, without the admission of some such element into the system. And, finally, that which to me gives this subject its supreme interest is the admitted necessity among scientists of the present time to assume, on mathematical and astronomical grounds, such as the character of light, the conservation of energy, the transmutation of force and the nebular hypothesis that there must be some such actual and potential agent through which the cosmic phenomena must be carried on and maintained.

This has not the tangible interest of a new fossil, it may be, but it is certainly a most curious and interesting preintimation of things to come.

Mr. Inman Horner, in the discussion that followed the paper, urged that modern thought on the subject of cosmic ether (and the correlation of forces) has a purely physical basis.

President Brinton, in commenting upon Dr. Garrison's address, which he characterized as highly erudite and suggestive, said that striking analogies in the same current of thought were found among the American Indians. They regarded light as the motor force of the universe. In the religion of the North American tribes the principle of light was regarded as the fundamental and most important principle of all. Not sun worship, or fire worship, as has been sometimes described, but the respect and worship of light. Among the Algonquins, according to the Jesuit Fathers, the highest divinities were those that made the light, *kichigouai*, "those that make the dawn." The great characters of the American hero myths may all be regarded as the personification of light—that something which is emitted by the sun, but not fire or the sun itself. The word *akasa*, that Dr. Garrison spoke of in the Upanishads, had its counterpart in the Mexican *Iloque nahuaque*, "that through and by which all things are." The general argument of Dr. Garrison, so far as it relates to the great development of man, is borne out by a study of the theology of the original inhabitants of America.

What one generation conceives in a mythological sense another may arrive at in a practical sense, but he did not understand the Greek philosophers, Anaximander and the rest, as having expressed the doctrine of evolution as we understand it. Among the Greeks there was a lack of any appreciation of organic development.

Mr. Stewart Culin, in referring to the existence of the idea of a cosmic ether among the people of the farther East, called attention to the argument presented by Gustave Schlegel in his work on "The Hung League," the great Chinese secret society, that an ancient worship of the principle of light is conserved in the institutions of that society

Mr. Robert S. Patterson presented a copy of the Eiffel Tower medal purchased by him on the highest stage of the tower. This medal was gilded, bronze and silver medals being sold on the first and second stages.

A committee consisting of Francis Jordan, Jr., Thomas Hockley, and John R. Baker was appointed to secure better accommodations for the meetings of the Society.

APRIL 3D.

Mr. Benjamin Smith Lyman read the following paper on

JAPANESE SWORDS.

The subject of Japanese swords, relics of barbarism as they are, is a rather unpromising one, and is, in fact, less fruitful than some others, but yet is not wholly without metallurgical, ethnological, historical, æsthetic, and even moral interest. In particular, anybody who happens to possess such a beautiful object, or to have the opportunity of inspecting one, is naturally desirous to learn something about it. Chiefly through the zeal and activity of our Secretary, Mr. Culin, we have a number of good specimens to exhibit this evening, lent by their owners for the occasion. There are :

Three swords belonging to Mr. Culin himself.

One sword belonging to the Baba collection, at Memorial Hall.

Two swords belonging to the University Museum.
One sword belonging to Mr. Terashima.
One sword belonging to Dr. McClure.
One sword belonging to Dr. Shober.
One sword, short, *heyazashi*, with dragon-flies on the scabbard, belonging to Mr. H. Rush Kirby.
Four swords belonging to myself.

No very full account of Japanese swords yet exists in English or is easily accessible in any language. A very thorough memoir on Japanese sword-blades is given by George Huetterott, Japanese Consul at Triest, in the Communications of the Japan German East Asiatic Society, Vol. IV, pp. 111–128, 1885. There are less complete articles on the Japanese sword by T. H. McClatchie, in the transactions of the Japan Asiatic Society, Vol. II, pp. 55–63, 1873; by C. Pfoundes, in *Fu-So-Mimi-Bukuro*, pp. 158–171, 1875; also, a paper by G. Mueller-Beeck, in the *Zeitschrift für Ethnologie*, 14 Jahrgang, 1882, Heft 1 (but I have not had any chance to see it); and swords are spoken of at some length in Mitford's *Tales of Old Japan*, Vol. I, pp. 70–73, and pp. 113, 114; and in Wertheimber's *A Muramasa Blade*.

The Japanese encyclopædia, *Wa-Kan-San-Sai-Dzu-E*, Vol. XXI, fol. 17, speaks of swords; also, other Japanese encyclopædic works.

Japanese swords may be discussed with reference to their own characteristics, their history, and the customs connected with them.

A. CHARACTERISTICS.

The characteristics of Japanese swords will best be learned by considering (1) their forms; (2) the processes of their manufacture; and (3) the methods of their valuation.

1. FORM.—According to the number of edges Japanese swords are divided into: (1) two-edged swords, called *tsurugi*; and (2) one-edged swords, called in general, *katana*.

1. *Tsurugi*.—The two-edged sword, called *tsurugi*, is the primeval form of sword in Japan, and for many centuries past has not been used, and is now seldom seen. It is set up as an ornament in temples. It was from 28 to 40 inches long, and about 2½ or 3 inches wide, and in the middle up to 3·5 of an inch thick. It ended in a short point, and often thickened and broadened towards the point. It was a heavy sword, and, though pointed, was for cutting more than for thrusting. (See figs. 1 and 2.)

It had two principal forms : (*a*) one flattened along the middle line, ending in an abrupt triangular point, and (*b*) the other sloping directly from the middle line to the edges, and with the point less abrupt.

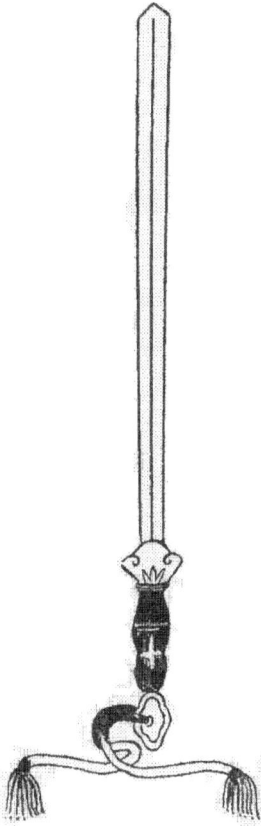

FIG. 1.—TSURUGI.   FIG. 2.—TSURUGI.

2. *Katana.*—The one-edged sword is supposed to have been derived from the *tsurugi* by division along its main line, with one edge, and is therefore, it is said, called *katana*, from *kata-no-ha* (*Wa-Kan-San-Sai-Dzu-E*, Vol. XXI, f. 17), or edge on (one) side. It became thereby more handy, and, in spite of its point, was still a cutting rather than a thrusting weapon, and was made yet more effective for cutting by a more or less decided curve. The superiority of swords fit for thrusting, and therefore straight and pointed, as weapons of

defense as well as offense, well known for centuries in Europe, and even understood by the ancients there, seems never to have been fully comprehended in Japan, nor in the rest of Asia. The defense has depended rather upon heavy armor. The Japanese, however, used lances for thrusting.

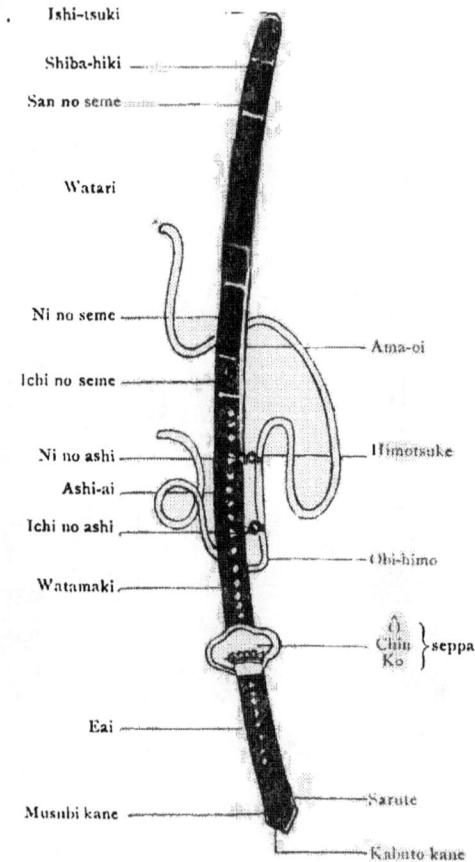

Ishi-tsuki
Shiba-hiki
San no seme
Watari
Ni no seme
Ichi no seme
Ni no ashi
Ashi-ai
Ichi no ashi
Watamaki
Eai
Musubi kane

Ama-oi
Himotsuke
Obi-himo
Ō Chiu Ko } seppa
Sarute
Kabuto kane

FIG. 3.—TACHI.

Of the one-edged swords there are many varieties of form with many ways of classifying them.

a. The most important kinds depend chiefly on the length, measured from the guard or inner end of the hilt to the point, as follows: *aa. Tachi; ab. Katana* proper; *ac. Wakisashi; ad. Tantō; ae. Yoroi-tōshi; af. Kuwaiken; ag. Kodzuka,* or *kami-kiri,* or *kogatana:* besides *ah,* several less important varieties.

aa. The *tachi* (fig. 3) is a sword said to be longer, more slender, and more strongly curved than the *katana* proper, and in some sort intermediate between it and the *tsurugi.* It is hung on by cords, or narrow straps or bands. It was the sword used by generals, and a sign of their rank. It has long been out of use, and is now somewhat rare and only seen as an ornament or curiosity.

ab. The *katana* proper (fig. 4) is on the average from 2 feet 6 inches

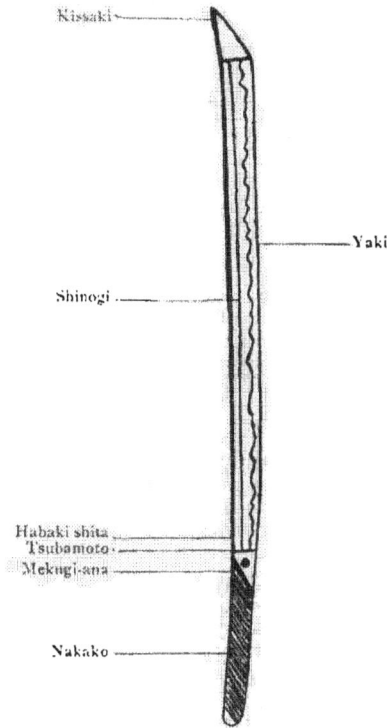

FIG. 4.—KATANA.

to 2 feet 9 inches long. It is the common long sword of Japan worn by the military class.

ac. The *wakizashi* averages about 1 foot 6 inches to 1 foot 8½ inches long, and has a guard between the hilt and blade. It is the shorter of the two swords worn by the military class.

ad. The *tantô* (*i. e.*, short sword) is somewhat shorter than the *wakizashi,* and is often "nine and a half tenths of a foot" (*ku-sun-go-bu*) long and so called. It was the sword allowed to be worn by tradesmen and others not allowed to wear the *katana* or *wakizashi*.

ae. The *yoroi-tôshi*, or mail-piercer, is a dagger still shorter than the *tantô;* and was formerly worn along with the *katana* and *waki-zashi*, before military men were restricted to these two.

af. The *kuwai-ken* is again a still shorter dagger worn by the ladies of the military class.

ag. The *kodzuka*, or *kamikiri* (paper cutter), or *kogatana* (little *katana*), is the small knife found inserted in the outer part of the scabbard of some *wakizashi*, *tantô*, and *yoroi-tôshi*. It ought, perhaps, not to be reckoned as a sword, though it has its warlike uses.

ah. There are several other forms distinguished by special names, but less commonly known, either because the varieties are more rare, or because the distinction is less important. Pfoundes enumerates several: the *jintachi* (war sword), a long, heavy two-handed sword, generally carried by a sword bearer when not in immediate use; the *nôdachi*, a more plainly-mounted sword of medium size, worn in hunting or in country rambles; the *shin-no-tachi*, a highly-ornamented *tachi*, with a shagreen hilt and some 75 examples of the owner's badge on the mountings; the *yô-no-tachi*, "with a lacquered and gilt scabbard," and corresponding perhaps to an *in-no-tachi*, as the *in* and *yô* are the male and female principles of the universe according to the Chinese philosophy; the *chisakatana* (small sword), about two feet or two feet and a half long, lighter than the ordinary *katana*, and worn with the long dragging trousers (*nagabakama*) of the court dress; the *aikuchi*, a short dagger, really a *tantô*, worn by doctors, artists, and others of a certain rank. There are also other names that are, perhaps, given to indicate special modes of wearing a sword rather than varieties of form, such as *metezashi*, a short sword stuck in the girdle behind, accessible to the right hand for use when the wearer is thrown and unable to draw the sword on the left; *mamori-katana* (protecting sword), a short dagger, or *tantô*, worn concealed. A very short sword, or short *tantô*, worn in the house is sometimes called a *heyazashi*.

b. Irrespective of length, one-edged sword blades may be distinguished according to their main cross-sections; and in correspondence with the *tsurugi* there are two principal varieties of cross-sections :

aa. The so-called proper-make (*hon-tsukuri*), or *shinogi*-make, having on each side of the blade two surfaces; one a flat surface, called *shinogi*, at right angles to the back, and from the back towards or to the mid-line; and a second called *jigane*, sloping thence down to the edge; the point, too, agrees with the corresponding form of the *tsurugi*, and generally is marked by a cross-line where it starts. The *shinogi* is distinguished as broad or narrow, and the point as small or large, or middling. Sometimes the edge is very narrow (called *kiri-ha*).

ab. The so-called plain make (*hira-tsukuri*), has no *shinogi*, only the *jigane* on each side of the blade, one surface sloping from the back to the edge, and is mostly confined to the shorter kinds of sword. The beginning of the slope towards the point is not marked by any cross-line. The point may either have its edge gently curving, almost straight (*fukura-sugu*), or more abruptly curving (*fukura-kaku*).

ac. According to the form of the back there are several varieties, as: (*aca*) Round-backed (*maru-mine*); (*acb*) angle-backed (*kaku-mine*); (*acc*) cormorant-neck-make (*u-no-kubi-tsukuri*), with a part of the back forming a blunt or cutting edge; (*acd*) with a slight difference also (called *kammuri-otoshi*); (*ace*) with such an edge all along the back or reaching nearly to the point, flag-leaf-make (*shōbu-tsukuri*).

ad. According to the grooves often cut in the blades, they are distinguished as: (*ada*) Groove-short-of-the-point (*hi-saki-shita*); (*adb*) groove-up-to-the-point (*hi-saki-ue*), and (*adc*) double-groove (*futa-suji-hi*).

ae. According to the general curve of the blade the swords are classed as: (*aea*) Nearly straight (*tsukuri-sugu*), and (*aeb*) strongly curved (*tsukuri-sori*).

1. MANUFACTURE.—The main features to be considered in the manufacture are: 1, the smith; 2, the material; and 3, the processes.

1. *Smith.* The swordsmith was held in high esteem, far above all other mechanics, and even one of the Emperors practiced the art of forging swords. Very good smiths were sometimes given the title of Lord or Vice-Lord of a province, or a high military rank, with an annuity. Some of our swords this evening are marked as made by the Lord of a province. The smith prepared himself for his work by prayers, by self-purification through the strictest fasting from all animal food and spirituous drink, through abstinence from all intercourse with women, even with his own wife, who was not allowed so much as to enter the forge, and through daily cold ablutions and other godly behavior of all kinds. Above the anvil, between two upright bamboos, hung the sacred straw-rope (*shime-nawa*), with its bunches of straw and its cut paper (*gohei*). The smith went to his important work adorned with the ceremonial

dress of a court noble. (See the picture in Mitford's *Tales of Old Japan*, Vol. I, p. 71.) With such manifold precautions the making of a blade often lasted months, or even years.

Not only must the five elements, fire, water, wood, metal, and earth, work together to make a good sword, but really great skill and experience was required. No doubt success was promoted by the profound concentrated attention, complete carefulness, and conscientious thoroughness aroused by the momentous solemnity attached to the operation through, to be sure, a superstition that gave it sanctity, so that the swordsmith

> " Wrought in a sad sincerity,
> Himself from God he could not free."

2. MATERIAL.—The earliest swords, *tsurugi*, were made of copper or bronze, but for many hundred years past only steel and iron have been used for them. The steel and iron were generally of Japanese origin,* but sometimes during the last three centuries European steel or iron has been used, obtained through the Dutch traders. Sometimes the sword is then marked as made of the iron of the *Namban* (Southern Barbarians), as Europeans were called Great care was taken in selecting a good quality, and numerous tests were made of the fracture during the early part of the forging.

The blade is sometimes made wholly of steel, and sometimes of steel and iron bars welded together. Sometimes an intimate mixture of steel and iron, half and half (in Sagami), or one-third steel and two-thirds iron (in Hizen), welded and hammered together, was used instead of the iron bars, thereby improving the quality; and sometimes instead of the steel ones, and so injuring the quality. The use of steel alone was called pure-make (*muku-tsukuri*), or pure-forging (*muku-gitai*). Often the mixed steel and iron plates were substituted for all the steel ones in this style.

3. PROCESSES.—The processes are :—(*a*) forging; (*b*) tempering; (*c*) the smith's finishing-up; (*d*) grinding; (*e*) mounting.

(*a*) *Forging.*—There are several styles of forging, mainly of two classes called (*aa*) pure-make; and (*ab*) mixed-make.

aa. Pure-make.—To begin with, the pure-make. Throughout the forging, the metal to prevent "burning," or the conversion of the steel into soft iron by the oxidation of its carbon, is never heated without being carefully coated with loam, as refractory as possible,

---

For the Japanese method of making steel and iron, see Appendix A.

spread over it as a thin wash and sprinkled with straw-ashes. The metal, too, is with the greatest pains kept perfectly clean, and must never be touched with the hand, as the least sweat will hinder the perfectly uniform welding of the parts together and leave a flaw visible in the sword.

A steel plate, with an iron rod welded to it as a handle, and with several pieces of steel placed upon it, is heated in the fire and is hammered out on the anvil to a shape about six or eight inches long by an inch and a quarter, or two and a half wide, and one-quarter or three-quarters of an inch thick, according to the size of the blade desired, allowing for loss in hammering. The steel bar so formed is marked with a chisel at mid-length, and doubled over, heated again, and hammered out to a bar of about the same dimensions as before ; doubled over again, re-heated and hammered out once more, and so on until it has been folded and hammered fifteen times. Then its iron handle is cut off. In like manner three more such bars are made. The four bars are welded upon one another into a somewhat thicker, longer bar, and this again is five times doubled over and hammered out to about the same dimensions.

The resulting bar, then, is made up of a vast number of layers intimately welded together. The first doubling gives two, the second four, and so on up to the fifteenth, which gives 32,768, and the four small bars together consist of 131,072 layers, and after the five additional foldings there must be 4,194,304 layers.

In consequence of these thin layers produced by the repeated folding, the polished sword has fine lines like the grain of wood. They are called the sword's *hada* (skin) ; and are distinguished, according to form, by the names straight-grain-skin (*masame-hada*, curved-grain-skin (*itame-hada*), like the grain of a board ; pear-skin (*nashi-hada*), in shape of a halved pear ; pine-skin (*matsu-hada*), ragged like the bark of a pine tree.

The steel bar is now with frequent and partial heating hammered out to the length of the desired blade ; somewhat bent in shape, if to be one-edged ; both ends cut off, where the metal is inferior ; the point formed, and by hammering thinner towards the edge (or in the case of the *tsurugi*, the two edges) the right breadth is obtained, and the blade gets its rough form. The shape is apparently given without measurements or patterns, but solely by the practiced skill of the smith with his true eye. The curve of one-edged swords depends on the taste of the smith or of the man who has ordered it, or in the case of certain ceremonial swords is prescribed by rules of etiquette.

The rough blade is scraped off with a kind of metal draw-knife and filed, and is then ready to have its edge hardened.

The shape of the file and the direction of the lines made with it have, of course, nothing to do with the quality of the sword. But, as the file lines (*yasuri-me*) remain permanently on the tang, they serve in some degree for the identification of the maker, and special names have been given to different arrangements of them. Among many, seven such names are given by Huetterott, p. 123 and plate xxvi.

The following nine names and illustrations of different kinds of file marks are taken from the *Yamato Setsuyô Daifuku :*

Fig. 5. *Higaki-yasuri ;* made by Seki, a family name, or perhaps at a place called Seki.

Fig. 6. *Kirisujikae-yasuri ;* made in the province Yamato.

Fig. 7. *Taka-no-ha ;* falcon's wing ; made in the province Yamato, by, or at, Seki.

Fig. 8. *Sujikae-yasuri ;* made in the province Bizen.

Fig. 9. *Sen-moku ;* made in the province Bitchiu.

Fig. 10. *Yoko-yasuri ;* made at Mihara.

Fig. 11. The file marks made at Awadakuchi, and sometimes found on swords made in the province of Etchiu.

Fig. 12. *Yoko-sujikae ;* made by Rai.

Fig. 13. *Katsura-yasuri-me ;* made at Kiyôto.

ab. Mixed-make.—When iron is used along with steel, there are several ways of combining the small bars to make the larger one. There are : the three-layer-make (*sam-mai-tsukuri*), a steel bar between two iron ones ; the folding-and-uniting-two-layer-make (*ori awase-ni-mai-tsukuri*), an iron bar welded upon a steel one and then folded over lengthwise with the steel inside ; the folding-and-uniting-three-layer-make (*ori-awase-sam-mai-tsukuri*), a bar of steel and of iron welded together along the edge and covered by an iron bar as wide as both, and then folded over so as to bring the steel in the middle of one edge. Then, three kinds that particularly show grain lines : the straight-grain-make (*masame-tsukuri*), an iron bar welded flatwise upon a steel one and folded fifteen times, then hammered down upon the long narrow side (where are the edges of the many layers) to the flat blade form again ; the fine-grain-make (*nogi-hada, or hasa-masame, or ko-masame-tsukuri*), like the preceding, only hammered down flat from one rectangular long edge towards the one diagonally opposite, the skin-forging (*hada-gitai*), with hollows cut by a chisel in the outer iron layers of the three-layer-make (*sam-mai-tsukuri*) and then hammered down again until the hollows have disappeared before giving the blade form. Then, the following three forms of wrapping iron in the steel with inferior results to the preceding: the over-turned-tortoise-shell-make (*ko-buse-tsukuri*), a small

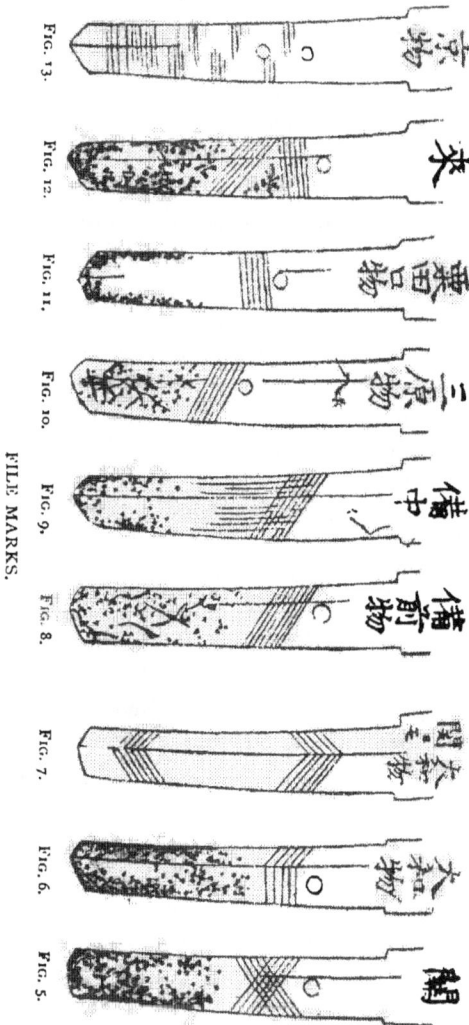

FILE MARKS.

FIG. 13.

FIG. 12.

FIG. 11.

FIG. 10.

FIG. 9.

FIG. 8.

FIG. 7.

FIG. 6.

FIG. 5.

bar of iron welded to the inner side of a semi-cylindrical bar of steel and then the steel made into the edge of the blade; the wrapping-up-make (*uchi-maki-tsukuri*), a steel bar welded upon an iron one and then folded lengthwise so as to bring the iron inside and

3

leave the steel outside along one edge ; the half-wrapping-make (*han-maki-tsukuri*), a narrower steel bar welded on an iron one and folded over lengthwise so as to leave the iron projecting from the steel at the back of the blade. Then :—three kinds more of very inferior quality but quicker to make, and frequent in war times—the four-side-packing-make (*shi-hô-dzume-tsukuri*), a bar of hard iron with one of soft iron welded along one edge, towards the back of the blade, and with a bar of steel along the edge, and with a broad bar of mixed steel and iron covering all three above and below ; the split-edge-make (*wari-ha-tsukuri*), a bar of iron split with a chisel along one edge and steel welded into it for the sword edge ; the applied-edge-make (*suc-ha-tsukuri*), a steel bar for the edge welded lengthwise to an iron bar for the back.

The foregoing thirteen varieties (including the pure-make) are the principal ones ; but other slighter variations might have been mentioned. Sometimes steel alone was used in all these different ways except in the split-edge and applied edge, and the work was then called genuine forging (*shin-no-kitai*), and valued accordingly.

In general, the pure-make and three-layer-make give the best blades, and the smiths of the provinces Bizen and Sagami preferably used those methods ; but the smiths of Yamashiro and Yamato used especially the straight-grain-make and the fine-grain-make. Still, it is not possible to draw a sharp line as to the methods used in different provinces, or by different famous smiths for the method is not to be distinguished' by inspecting the surface of the finished blade, except perhaps in the split-edge and the applied-edge. Some assert that it can be told in the fracture, but that is somewhat doubtful and the opportunity seldom occurs with swords of celebrated masters.

b. TEMPERING.—The tempering of the sword is ingeniously and skillfully effected by a single operation in Japan instead of the two common in Western countries. In preparation for the tempering the blade is covered with a coating of loam about an eighth of an inch thick. The loam must stand the fire well, and is mostly a red earth, called rust-mud (*sabi-doro*), mixed with other things ; commonly with an equal quantity of the finest powdered river-sand and one-tenth of the finest powdered charcoal. Many swordsmiths keep the composition secret.

Before the loam coating is quite hard, a narrow streak of it is very carefully removed with a bamboo rod along the edge of the blade, so as to leave the edge bare. The rest, completely covering all the other parts of the blade, is dried by the fire.

The smith in his right hand holds the blade by the handle with pincers and thrusts it edge downwards horizontally into the hottest part of a strong fire of pine charcoal of a special quality called forge-coal, while his assistant, or he himself with his left hand, regulates the heat by the bellows. The blade is moved slowly backwards and forwards in order to be uniformly heated throughout its whole length. The part next the tang is often drawn slowly out of the fire so that the master's practiced eye may judge in the carefully closed and darkened smithy when the right degree of heat has arrived. It comes in a few minutes; and the sooner the better, so that the loam covering may not have time to get overheated through and through.

The blade is taken from the fire and plunged immediately into cool lukewarm water, of a temperature and during a time determined by the smith, each smith his own way. The sudden chilling hardens the bare edge, and makes it capable of great sharpness, though very brittle. The loam protects the rest of the blade from too great heat in the fire, and now from too sudden chilling in the water, and so the desired temper for the body of the sword, sufficient hardness with toughness and elasticity, is obtained by the same operation that gives the still greater hardness to the edge.

This kind of hardened edge is called baked-edge (*yaki-ba*); and is readily distinguished by its lighter, whitish color, "edge-lustre" (*ha-tsuya*) from the darker, bluish color, "ground-lustre" (*ji-tsuya*) of the rest of the blade.

The narrow strip left bare at the edge for hardening is not always of the same breadth or shape, but differs according to fancy, and thereby many varieties with special names are distinguished. Huetterott enumerates about thirty of the principal ones (p. 121 and plates xxiii–xxv). A very broad *yaki-ba* is, however, not desirable, as it implies that a large breadth of the blade is brittle. Consequently a narrow straight hardened edge (*sugu-ha*), or simple irregular one (*midare-ha*), is in general preferred, and of most frequent occurrence. Among the other forms there is no special preference, and they are no indication of the quality of the sword. They are determined by the fancy of the smith or of the man who ordered the sword, and depend somewhat on fashion. In times of long peace the more complicated forms are apt to be preferred. The form is not a mark by which the celebrated smiths' work can be absolutely distinguished, as each used various forms, yet connoisseurs know which forms occur most frequently in the work of the different masters.

The bounding line of the hardening at the point of the blade likewise gives rise to many various forms and names. Huetterott enumerates eight (see page 122 and plate xxvi).

The bath causes a curved sword to bend in some degree further; and that depends partly on the manner of plunging the blade into the water. A straight sword is dipped vertically downwards; a curved one is let down horizontally into the water, with the edge down, either suddenly or slowly, either evenly or with the point slightly lower at first and rising from the water as the tang goes in. This bending from the bath may amount in the case of a sword 32 inches long to as much as an inch and a fifth. If the blade curves too much, or by bad holding bends sidewise, it can be heated and hammered again, but with no benefit to the quality.

c. SMITH'S FINISHING-UP.—After the tempering, the blade is carefully cleaned, and is roughly ground on a coarse stone. The smith then first sees whether the blade is a success or not; whether the hardening is satisfactory, and whether there are blemishes in the metal. A smith careful of his reputation rejects all imperfect blades, and uses the material for other purposes. A less strict smith would let such failures be sold secretly and cheaply, but perhaps not under his own name.

Next, the smith cuts the grooves, if any, with a steel graving tool. The groove must have an exactly semi-circular cross-section. The grooves lighten the sword, and are found in even the oldest *tsurugi* and *katana*, and are called *hi*, and vulgarly *chi-nagashi* (blood drains), and were often filled with vermilion lacquer on lance points, though that was not thought fine for swords.

The smith drills the hole (*mekugi-ana*) in the tang for the bamboo or metallic peg that holds the handle on.

Many smiths adorn their blades with engraving, especially with representations of dragons, gods, flower-sprigs, etc. Some blades have Chinese, or *hiragana* characters, single words or whole sentences, or sometimes Sanscrit letters—sacred letters (*bonji*), as a charm. Such adornments sometimes serve to conceal blemishes in the blade, and consequently are little liked by some connoisseurs. The fine, short sword of Dr. Shober, exhibited at a former meeting, had on its blade a word in *hiragana* characters—*Osoraku* (fearful), apparently the name of the sword. One of the swords this evening has a dragon and some god on it.

The smith sometimes cuts his name on the tang, and the custom existed as long as about twelve hundred years ago, beginning, probably, with the swordsmith Amakuni of the period Taihô (A. D. 701-

703), according to the encyclopædia called Yamato-Setsuyô-Daifuku etc., but has often been left unfollowed. Poor swords have commonly no maker's name, but it is related of some of the most famous makers— for example, Masamune and Yoshihiro—that they would not put their name on a sword, because anybody that understood swords at all would recognize theirs by the quality. With the name on the tang is often given the title and the date, and sometimes the name of the man who ordered the blade; and the name of the sword itself, if it already had one when forged; and again, pithy sayings, or wishes, or poems.

Among the swords here this evening, the long one with the orange-colored scabbard is marked on one side of the tang: "*Idzumo no Kami Fujiwara Yoshitake,*" i. e., "Fujiwara (clan-name) Yoshitake (*nanori*, a personal name), Lord of (the province) Idzumo." On the other side of the tang is written: "*Motte shisubeshi, motte ikubeshi. Inkiyô, Gan, Kô Shi. Kawachi Kusuba no hito, Nakai Mototaka obu;* i. e., " Should die with (it), should live with (it). A. D. 1744. A man of Kusuba, (in the Province) Kawachi, Nakai (family name) Mototaka (*nanori*) wears (it)." On the tang of the short sword with leather-covered scabbard is written: "*Wakasa no Kami Ujifusa, Kei-Chô, yo nen san guwatsu—hi;*" i. e., " Ujifusa (*nanori*), Lord of (the Province) Wakasa. A. D. 1599, third month, — day," on the tang of the very short sword (*heyazashi*), with dragon-flies on the scabbard, is written: "*Wakasa no Kami, Fujiwara Ujiyoshi,*" i. e., "Fujiwara (clan-name) Ujiyoshi (*nanori*), Lord of Wakasa." On the tang of Mr. Culin's long sword is written: "*Bizen (no) Kuni (no) sumi Osafune Katsumitsu,*" i. e., "Bizen province inhabitant, Osafune (family name) Katsumitsu (*nanori*)." But Osafune appears by the next sword to be mentioned to be the name of a place. On the tang of a sword formerly owned by Mr. Tatsui Baba is written: "*Bizen Osafune jû Yokoyama Sukekane,*" i. e., "Bizen (province) Osafune (town) inhabitant, Yokoyama (family name) Sukekane (*nanori*)." On the tang of my long sword is written: "*Empô San, Etsu U, ku guwatsu, kichinichi. Geishiu jû Kanesaki kore(o) tsukuru,*" i. e., "A. D. 1675, ninth month, lucky day. Aki province inhabitant Kanesaki (*nanori*)."

It should be remembered that inscriptions of makers' names are sometimes counterfeited, though not without some slight variations; yet so that a confirmation from other signs is important.

Sometimes the tang shows that the sword has been shortened, since it was first made; for example, to accommodate the shorter stature of one who has inherited it. That fact is nothing against the quality of the sword.

d. GRINDING.—The final grinding and polishing of the sword is a trade quite distinct from the smith's. The grinder holds the sword horizontally before him with both hands, protected by cloths wound about the blade, with a narrow piece of the blade uncovered between. He rubs it back and forth on a small whetstone, well wet with water, moving by degrees through the whole length of the blade, except the tang; first, with coarser stones, then with finer, up to four, six, or eight for ordinary work, or, for very fine work, fifteen stones; giving to it many days, and even weeks, as well as great patience, skill, and care. The Japanese whetstones are of excellent quality, and of numerous varieties.

Finally, the blade is polished with a polishing-stone and with a stone-powder as fine as flour, or with the finest powdered steel-forge cinder and oil, as well as with a small, round rod of wrought iron (*migaki-hari*) until the polish is perfect.

The cross-section of the blade should be left convex on both sides; if too thin, or concave on both sides, the edge is easily broken.

Every sword needs a slight grinding from time to time, and the selection of a good grinder is very important; and some grinders have great reputations.

Winter is preferred to summer for polishing, as newly-polished swords are thought to rust too easily in summer.

e. MOUNTING.—The blade may now be mounted with a hilt, and if at least moderately long, with a guard, with a ferrule (*habaki*), and with a scabbard; and the scabbard has certain fittings.

ea. HILT.—The hilt (*tsuka*) is made of wood, often covered with shark-skin, the rougher the better; sometimes with leather. (Fig. 14.) Over the shark-skin silk cord (*tsuka-ito*) is often bound crosswise in several styles (*maki, dashi-me-nuki, katate-maki, hiyo-maki*, etc.). Between the shark-skin and the silk there is often a metallic ornament (*me-nuki*) on either side of the hilt, near the middle, but not exactly opposite each other; apparently useful also for further security of grasp. Sometimes, instead of the silk, there is open-work iron with slightly corrugated surface. The hilt has a small hole (*mekugi-ana*) through it, so as to be held to the tang by a peg (*mekugi*) of bamboo, or by a metallic rivet, that has sometimes a small ornament over each end. The hilt has at its outer end a ferrule (*tsuka-kashira*) of iron, or of some more valuable metal or alloy. There is also a metallic ferrule (*fuchi-kashira*) at the end of the hilt, towards the guard. It is sometimes made highly ornamental, and may have its maker's name inscribed on the part that is hidden. For example: the *fuchi-kashira* of my long sword bears the maker's names, as follows: "Gakô-Shi (*gô*, or pen-name) Minamoto (clan-name) Nagayoshi (*nanori*)," and

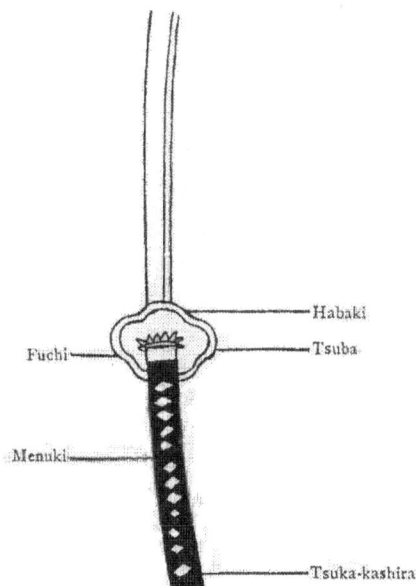

FIG. 14.—THE HILT (TSUKA).

then his *kaki-han*, or written seal, a kind of monogram constructed of abbreviated characters.

The owner of several sword-blades sometimes has one hilt serve for more than one of them, by turns; so that in the case of Mr. Baba's

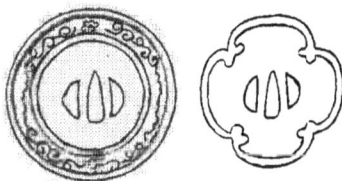

FIG. 15.—THE GUARD (TSUBA).

sword here to-night there is only a rough, unvarnished hilt and scabbard, to protect it from rust while not in use.

eb. GUARD.—The guard (*tsuba*) is put upon the *wakizashi* and larger swords, but not on the shorter ones. (See fig. 15.) It is made, preferably for use, of steel or the hardest wrought-iron; but for ornament other metals are used, and on some very small swords it is made of wood. It is sometimes a work of fine art, and then often has its maker's name engraved upon the concealed part of it; of course, quite a different man from the smith who made the blade.

On either side of the guard there is a metallic washer (*seppa*), and

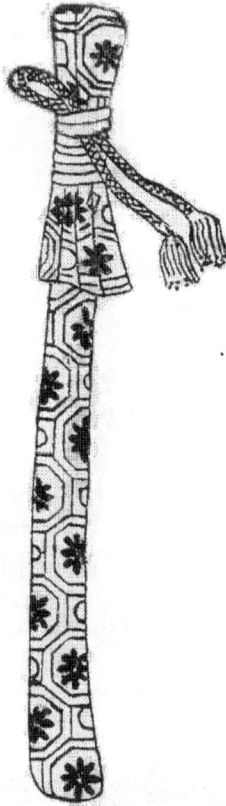

FIG. 16.

sometimes two, a thicker one (*ôseppa*) and a thinner one (*koseppa*); and perhaps also one of middling thickness (*chiuseppa*). One of Mr. Culin's short swords has the name of the maker (*Hisanori*) of the *tsuba* inscribed on the *seppa*. The *seppa* is sometimes wanting on short swords.

cc. HABAKI.—Next to the guard the blade is covered with a metallic ferrule (*habaki*) about an inch long; sometimes, but not always, of the same metal as the *seppa*.

ed. SCABBARD.—The scabbard (*saya*) is made of the wood of the Magnolia hypoleuca (*ho-no-ki*), a wood that is considered to be specially suited to the purpose and incapable of scratching the sword. (See fig. 17.) Outside, the scabbard is generally lacquered, preferably with black or dark colors ; sometimes with gaudy crimson and variegated colors ; sometimes with peculiar lacquer, and sometimes inlaid with mother of pearl. Sometimes handsomely lacquered scabbards are protected by leather covers, or with brocade bags. (See fig. 16.) Some scabbards are immediately covered with leather. A plain, un-

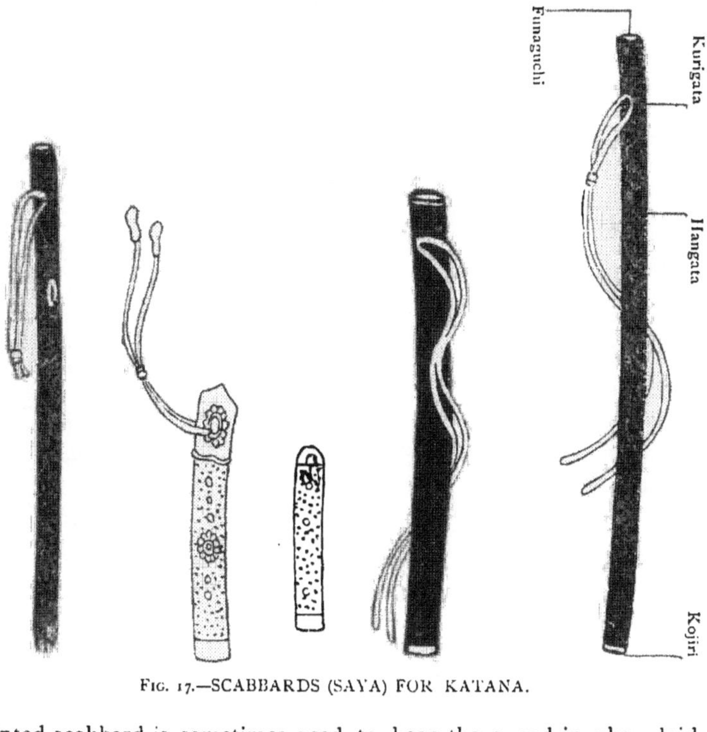

FIG. 17.—SCABBARDS (SAYA) FOR KATANA.

painted scabbard is sometimes used to keep the sword in when laid away (for instance, Mr. Baba's sword and my long sword).

eda. The scabbard has a metallic ferrule (*kojiri*) at its lower end, often very ornamental. (See fig. 17.)

edb. The scabbard also has a small projecting eye (*kurigata*) about two or three inches below its top (see fig. 17) to hold the silken cord, or braid (*sage-o*), with which the scabbard is sometimes slung over the shoulder. The cord is also used for tying up the loose, flowing Japanese sleeves in fighting. The scabbard of the *tachi* requires two projections for the cords or bands, by which it is hung. (See fig. 18.)

edc. Outside the scabbard, near its upper end, there is commonly inserted a small metallic skewer (*kôgai*), if there be no guard ; and sometimes, if there be one, it passes through a hole in it. Sometimes the *kôgai* is split lengthwise into two parts (*wari-kôgai*). The skewer is used in the heat of battle to stick through the ear into the head of a slain foe, for the purpose of identification afterwards. Also, the head of the enemy can be carried by it for presentation to the victor's lord. The skewer is sometimes of steel, with sharp edges and

FIG. 18.—SCABBARD FOR TACHI.

point, and can be used as a paper-knife. The split *kôgai* can be used on an emergency as chopsticks in eating food.

Such a pair that we have here this evening is made of the alloy called *shakudô* (see appendix B), and bear a Japanese poem inscribed on them as follows :

Yama mo saku
Umi mo arananu
Yo nari to mo
Ugoki wa seji na
Yamato damashii !

The inscription was probably made when the old conservative patriotic spirit was urging with much excitement the expulsion of foreigners, twenty or thirty years ago. It means very literally: Though even the mountain-itself-rending sea's real condition exist; as for moving, not (so) doing (is) the Japanese spirit. Or:

> Though mountain-rending seas assault the land,
> The Japanese staunch spirit firm shall stand.

cdd. In the outside of the scabbard likewise is often inserted a small knife (*kodzuka*), sometimes called a paper-cutter (*kamikiri*), or simply a little sword (*kogatana*). It is used, as a last resource, to throw at the enemy in battle, and also to cut his throat to make sure of his death when he is down and nearly dead. Its more peaceful use is to cut holes in sheets of paper that need to be bound together, as almost daily happens in Japan. Its blade is a poorly fashioned knife, according to our notions, and is commonly ill-polished and rusty with neglect. It is sometimes inscribed with its maker's name, apparently the maker also of the sword. For example, one of Mr. Culin's short swords has on the blade of the paper-knife the following inscription: "*Hizen no Kami Fujiwara Kuninaga;*" *i. e.,* "Fujiwara (clan-name) Kuninaga (*nanori*), Lord of Hizen." Also on the blade of the paper-cutter of my short sword (*wakizashi*) with a black scabbard is written: "*Tashiro Genichi Kanemoto tsukuru;*" *i. e.,* "Tashiro (family name) Genichi (*namae*, or childhood name) Kanemoto (*nanori*) made it." On the blade of the small knife of my other short sword (*wakizashi*) is written: "*Fujiwara Naoyuki,*" the maker's clan-name and *nanori.*

The paper-knife has often a very ornamental metallic handle; and such handles by themselves are now well known in America and applied to other knives.

III. VALUATION.—The value of a sword-blade may be ascertained —1, by actual test of its powers; and 2, by inspection of the signs of its quality.

1. TESTS.—It appears to be customary to test the newly-made sword only by trial upon the corpses of beheaded convicts; or by having them used in the execution itself; or ruffians sometimes used to try a new sword upon beggars or unmartial wayfarers; or even it was tried on a dog, though the use of a sword against brute animals was scouted at.

Huetterott, in the zeal of his thorough investigation of swords, sacrificed a couple of good ones in trying them upon metal. With one good blade of Mino he cut open with one blow, without injury to the edge, five *Tempô* coins piled one on another; in all a full half-inch of thickness of bronze, and an inch and a quarter wide. The same sword struck upon a piece of hard wrought-iron about a quarter of an inch thick and over half an inch wide, cut about an eighth of an inch deep and became notched. At a second stronger blow it cut about the same depth and broke in two at the point struck. A good Satsuma blade could only cut through four *Tempô*, and broke at the third blow on the wrought-iron after getting large notches by the two other blows without cutting very deep; but an inferior Kiyôto sword that could only cut through three *Tempô* endured three blows on the wrought-iron. It may be added that English military swords are tested, when made, by a violent blow on a solid block, with the two sides flat, with the edge, and lastly with the back; then it is bent flatwise in both directions by hand, and finally thrust through a steel plate about an eighth of an inch thick; and about forty per cent. fail to bear the test and are rejected.

2. SIGNS OF QUALITY.—Connoisseurs, and more particularly sword-grinders, with their long experience and close observation of swords in grinding, are extremely, almost incredibly, skillful in detecting the signs of the quality of a blade, and in recognizing the make of the numerous different celebrated masters. The most famous connoisseurs belong to the sword-grinding family of Honnami, who have been the imperial sword appraisers for the past 550 years. The most famous was Honnami Kotoku, in the middle of the 16th century. Honnami Chukei was in 1885 (and perhaps still is) the official representative of the family, and had the skill to decide authoritatively and beyond a question the origin of a sword, as Huetterott found by as many as twenty trials. The official appraisers under the former government had the sole right to make out certificates in regard to swords, writing them on a folded sheet (*orikami*) of special paper (*Kaga-bôsho*), rough large sheets made in Kaga, of which he received 100 sheets a year from the government.

The form of a blade and its point often gives a clue to its origin. What is more difficult, the quality of the metal, as shown by the particles on the surface of the well-polished blade, may also give some clue to the province and age of the sword.

The appearance of the *yakiba* (baked edge) has an important bearing on the quality. Though the more distinct are its whitish color and the bluish of the rest of the blade, the better the metal and its forging; yet the limit between the two colors should not be hard and sharp, but softly bounded, which is partly caused by a weak, cloudy glimmer in irregular spots (called *nioi*) along the union of the brighter hardened and the dark unhardened portions. Partly in the one, often to the very edge, and partly in the other, they are found in all blades, and only in a very poor blade are rare. They arise during the hardening, and in various number and character according to the quality of the metal and of the forging and to the temperature of the last heating; and cannot be counterfeited. It is in general thought well that they should not be uniformly scattered, but in thicker and thinner groups, like the clouds in the sky. Grouped in larger spots, they are called *nioi-buka*. See Huetterott's plate xxiv.

If the loam covering, while moving the blade back and forth during the heating, becomes thinner in some spots or loose, so that the heat of the fire and subsequently the chilling of the bath work more strongly, there arise in the surface of the blade isolated cloudy spots called *tobi-yaki* or *yu-hashiri*. They cannot be produced on purpose, are rare, and are seen with satisfaction.

The "grain" on the surface of good swords should be soft and tender, "as if water rippled over the metal."

A certain degree of heat very favorable for the hardening, as well as especial success in the chilling, produces on the surface of the lighter colored hardened edge very minute shining points called *nie*. According to some they arise from bubbling in the water. They are often very difficult to perceive, and sometimes even a connoisseur requires a magnifying glass to discern them. They are reckoned a sign of good quality, and occur on most of the better blades, and especially in large number on Masamune's. Large *nie* are called *ara-nie*.

On many, though not all, good blades, and especially on those of Bizen, but never on bad blades, there appears a weak glimmer, called *utsuri* (not to be confounded with the *nioi*), running parallel to the hardened edge inside the darker metal, "like the colors of the rainbow and the halo of the moon."

Huetterott learned to detect all the foregoing signs, but was unable to perceive still others that the connoisseurs described, as follows:

Chikei, weak, quite small cloud specks or points along the boundary of the hardened edge; in appearance like *nioi*, in shape like *nie*.

Inadzuma (lightning) extremely fine shining lines in the *nioi* spots.

Suna-gashi, such lines but formed of countless minute points, "like marks on sand that has been swept."

Uchi-yoke, a narrow local glimmer at the border of the hardened edge, similar to the *utsuri*.

Neither the quality nor the quantity of any one of all these signs is decisive, but rather their combination.

As regards the money value of a fine sword, Mitford, in 1871, says, nobles sometimes wore blades "worth unmounted from £200 to £300," say $1,000 to $1,500. Of course, since the wearing of swords has been forbidden the demand for them and their price have greatly fallen.

B.—HISTORY.

The history of swords may be considered, 1, in a general way, and 2, illustrated by lists of famous sword-makers.

1. GENERAL.—One name given by the Japanese to Japan is the land of many blades, and it is claimed that the first sword (*tsurugi*) was invented by the same god that invented poetry (perhaps a compensation). A certain god struck the eight-clawed great dragon on the tail, nicking the sword, but drew out of the tail a marvelous blade that was called the Clustering-cloud sword, and that was made one of the Mikado's three divine insignia (curved jewel, sword, and mirror). It was also called (see *Anderson's Catalogue of Japanese Paintings*, etc., p. 141) *Kusanagi no Tsurugi*, or the Grass-cutting Falchion, because Yamatodake, son of the Emperor Keikô (A. D. 71–130) used it to cut the grass around him when his barbarian enemies tried to burn him up at the foot of Mount Fuji. At length the tenth mortal Emperor Suijin Tennô (A. D. 192) is said to have had it deposited in a temple, keeping for himself an imitation made by the first recorded human swordsmith, Amakuni of Uda in Yamato. But the oldest known swords, some of them still extant, were made by another smith of the same name and place, apparently the first authentic swordsmith of Japan, about A. D. 702. He already made one-edged swords (*katana*).

The Emperor Gotoba-In, who came to the throne in 1184, greatly favored the art of sword-making and even practiced it himself. The art flourished especially in the 13th and 14th centuries, the age of the best swords, up to the present time. In general the art flourished in times of many wars. For the past three hundred years, since the beginning of the last dynasty of Shôguns, Japan has been mainly at peace and skill in sword-making has somewhat declined. The term old swords is (or used to be) applied only to swords made before this long peaceful period—that is, before 1603.

Until 1682 (*Wakansansaidsue*, vol. 21, fol. 17) it appears that there was no restriction in regard to the number of swords worn by anybody, and that it was common for military men to wear three swords, including the short dagger, called the mail-piercer (*yoroi-tooshi*), besides the *katana* and *wakizashi*. In that year the law was made that military men should wear the *katana* and *wakizashi*, but that farmers, mechanics, and merchants should only wear one *tantō* (dagger). About 1874 it was forbidden to the public to wear swords at all; after a few years of permitted neglect of the custom.

2. FAMOUS SWORD-MAKERS.—McClatchie says the four most famous sword-makers seem to be Munechika (A. D. 900–1000), Yoshimitsu (about 1275), Masamune (about 1290), and Muramasa (about 1340). The most celebrated of these is Masamune and next to him perhaps Muramasa, one of his pupils. For further lists see Huetterott, pp. 115 and 116. The *Yamato Setsuyō Daifuku* gives, with illustrations, the names of a number of the more celebrated makers, and marks by which their swords may be recognized.

C.—CUSTOMS.

The customs in regard to swords may be spoken of under the heads of: 1, their use; 2, their etiquette, and 3, customary beliefs or superstitions in regard to them.

I. USE.—The use of swords consists in, 1, the way of wearing them; 2, swordsmanship or fence; and 3, the care of them when out of direct use.

1. *Wearing.*—The swords are worn in the girdle with the edge upwards and the hilt inclined somewhat towards the right. The shorter swords, without guards, can also be worn concealed in the bosom. The name *kuwai-ken* for ladies' swords implies that they are worn in the bosom; but I saw one, about 1874, worn openly in the girdle as an adornment at a festive gathering.

2. *Fence.*—There are various styles of fencing, and in some of them some attention is paid to thrusting and to protecting the body by keeping the sword before it. Still, with the curved sword, cutting is the principal use, and the body is left much exposed. It is unnecessary here to go into details in regard to the different modes of fencing.

The *tantō* or *ku-sun-go-bu*, or dagger, when grasped with the thumb towards the outer end of the hilt and held up with the edge more or less nearly parallel to the forearm, is said to be an effective weapon against even the long *katana*.

The *wakizashi* was used in the ceremonious suicide by disembowelling (*seppuku* or *hara-kiri*). The *katana* was used in beheading criminals.

3. *Care of Swords.*—Swords ought to be carefully oiled and rubbed from time to time, the Japanese say as often as once in six months, and in the case of very valuable swords perhaps once a month. Otherwise moisture from the air condenses upon them and produces rust. Above all they ought not to be kept uncovered by a scabbard of some kind. Occasionally in the course of years they should be slightly reground.

II. ETIQUETTE.—Some Japanese have said, according to McClatchie, that men of high birth wore the sword so that the hilt pointed straight upwards, almost parallel with the body, while the common people stuck it horizontally in the belt, and ordinary military men wore it in a position about half way between those two. He further says: To draw a sword from its scabbard without begging leave of the others present was not thought polite; to clash the scabbard of your sword against another was a great rudeness; to turn the sword in the scabbard, as if about to draw, was tantamount to a challenge, and to lay your weapon on the floor and kick the guard towards another was an intolerable insult that generally resulted in a combat to the death.

Pfoundes says that "the rules of observances connected with the wearing of the long and short sword or the single sword are most minute, but have fallen into disuse. . . . In former days the most trivial breach of these minute observances was often the cause of murderous brawls and dreadful reprisals. . . . To express a wish to see a sword was not usual, unless, when a blade of great value was in question; and then a request to be shown it would be a compliment appreciated by the happy possessor. The sword would then be handed with the back towards the guest, the edge turned towards the owner and the hilt to the left, the guest wrapping the hilt either in the little silk napkin always carried by gentlemen in their pocket-books, or in a sheet of clean paper. The weapon was drawn from the scabbard and admired inch by inch, but not to the full length unless the owner pressed his guest to do so, and then, with much apology, the sword was entirely drawn and held away from the other persons present. After being admired, it would, if apparently necessary, be carefully wiped with a special cloth, sheathed and returned to the owner as before."

A guest, on entering a friend's house, if the host was an older man or of higher rank, would take off his longer sword and either lay it down at the entrance or hand it to the servant who admitted him, and who would place it on the sword rack in the place of honor in the parlor. If on somewhat familiar or equal terms with the host, the guest might carry the long sword into the house detached with its scabbard from the belt and lay it on the floor at his right hand, where it could not be drawn. "The shorter sword was retained in the girdle; but in a prolonged visit both host and guest laid it aside."

Miss A. M. Bacon, in her excellent book on *Japanese Girls and Women*, Boston, 1891, says, p. 201: "To use a sword badly, to harm or injure it, or to step over it, was considered an insult to its owner."

Many gentlemen of importance had their long sword carried for them, in the house, or at other times when not needed, by a boy or a young woman, who knelt or stood a short distance behind him to one side and held the sword in its scabbard upright. "On journeys the gentleman's sword-bearer carried the honored blade covered with a sword case (*shiki-hada*) of leather or cloth emblazoned with the owner's badge."

III. SUPERSTITIONS.—It is often said that Masamune's swords are so fine that they will cut a hair falling in the air; or cut in two the very hard-skinned adzuki bean as it falls; or if held in a stream will cut in two a sheet of paper floating down. Mitford relates (vol. I, p. 113) that "the swords of Muramasa are said to be so finely tempered as to cut hard iron like a melon, yet have the reputation of being unlucky, and are supposed to hunger after taking men's lives, and to be unable to repose in their scabbard. . . . They madden their owners, so that they either kill others indiscriminately or commit suicide. At the end of the 16th century, Tokugawa Ieyasu was in the habit of carrying a spear made by Muramasa with which he often scratched or cut himself by mistake. Hence the Tokugawa family avoid girding on Muramasa blades, which are supposed to be specially unlucky to their race. The murders of Gompachi, who wore a sword by this maker, also contributed to give his weapons a bad name.

"The swords of Tôshirô Yoshimitsu, on the other hand, are specially auspicious to the Tokugawa family, for the following reason: Ieyasu, after a certain defeat, wished to commit hara-kiri with a dagger he wore, made by Yoshimitsu; but, to his surprise, the blade turned aside. Thinking it must be a bad one, he tried it on a physician's iron mortar that happened to be at hand, and the point entered and transfixed the mortar; so he was once more about to stab himself, when his followers discovered him, took away his dagger, set him on a horse, and compelled him to flee to his own province. After that, he became *Shōgun*, and, ever since, Yoshimitsu's blades have been considered lucky in the family.''

There is a legend that Masamune in forging his swords kept time to his hammer blows with the cry, '' Tenka taihei ! Tenka taihei !'' (Peace on earth ! Peace on earth !) and his swords accordingly were always used with good omen and with peaceful results. But that Muramasa in like manner kept time with the cry, ''Tenka tairan ! Tenka tairan !'' (War on earth ! War on earth !) so that his swords were never satisfied without causing mischief, and could not be returned to the scabbard without drawing blood. There is, indeed, a saying that the swords of Muramasa must never be drawn and returned to the scabbard without making blood flow.

It is said a certain celebrated swordsmith went by the name of '' the one-handed smith.'' He had apprenticed himself to a famous swordsmith and learned from him the whole art of swordmaking, except that the master concealed the precise temperature of the water used in tempering. At length the pupil stealthily watching, burst into the forge and plunged his hand into the water at the very moment the master was about to dip the sword into it. The master with the sword instantly cut off the pupil's hand.

Certain swords have names, as already mentioned, and as occurred formerly in Europe, for example : Excalibur. McClatchie says a sword of great repute in the Taira family was called Little Crow. Last year we spoke of the historic sword that was called Higekiri (the beard-cutter), because when tried in beheading a criminal it cut through the beard at the same blow ; and we mentioned, too, that other historic sword called Hizamaru (the knee-sword), because at a like trial it cut through the knee ; also the sword in the romance of the *Eight Dogs of Satomi* called *Murasame* (autumn showers), from its magical shedding of water that washed it clean from blood. We have here this evening the sword inscribed with its name, Osoraku, in large hiragana letters on its blade.

'' Live with it, die with it,'' was a true saying ; for the sword was the constant companion of the military man, and closely identified with his whole life, with his power to gain a livelihood, and make his life respected, with the defense of his own and his family's good name, of his lord and of his country, with the most highly-honored death possible to him, and perhaps above all, with the savage ideas of the vendetta that persisted in Japan until very recent years—to avenge, however, be it said, rather injury to a master or parent than to himself. It naturally happened, then, as with other men who are closely bound to some inanimate object, as the sailor to his ship, the engine-driver to his locomotive, and the like, that the sword acquired almost personality, and became the centre, not only of attachment, but warm affection. It was so reverenced, indeed, that in the document Ieyasu left for the guidance of his successors he says: "The sword is the knight's living soul."

Happily, however, such progress in civilization is now taking place in Japan that we may expect soon to see the gross notions of the vendetta and other kindred forms of violence that are almost unavoidably inseparable from a universal habit of carrying deadly weapons, as strongly discountenanced there, as they long have been in Western countries, and to find the Japanese sword regarded in its own country as an emblem of rude savagery, as well as of unenlightened military art.

THE JAPANESE METHOD OF MAKING STEEL AND IRON.

Extracts from B. S. L.'s Report of Progress of the Geological Survey of Japan, for 1878, page 59 (published at Tokio, in 1879).

In the region about Minari [in the province of Idzumo] there are eight iron-making places, of which, however, only three seem to be working, namely at Amegawa, a league and a quarter easterly from Minari ; Une, the same distance southeasterly from Minari ; and Makibara. . . . I went from Minari to the Amegawa works ; and Mr. Adachi to those of Une, which I also visited on my way back. . . .

The iron ore used at all the works is [magnetic] iron sand ; and is obtained either by cutting down the granite and breaking it up by hand and washing it ; or the river sand is washed ; or the ore is taken from alluvial ground. The ore from such alluvium is reddish and more fusible than the other kinds, owing no doubt to its long exposure to weathering influences ; the ore washed from the rock is next in fusibility ; and the ore separated from river sand is the least fusible, probably owing to its being protected by water from the air, or because its weathered surface has been continually worn off. The difficult fusibility is very likely due in part to the presence of titanium. Most of the ore used at Amegawa is brought on horseback from various places over two leagues distant ; but is washed again at the furnace and reduced to half its weight. Some ore, however, is washed on the hill-side close by the Amegawa furnace in the winter half of the year, but the rock there is reckoned in general of inferior quality, though some parts are pretty good. Six men work together in one place and produce 800 to 1,000 loads, sometimes only 600 loads (of 24 kamme or 1½ piculs each) in one season of about 180 days, or 1,080 days work ; and that amount of ore is likewise reduced one-half by the final washing at the furnace. In one such season, it is said, the six men cut down and wash the rock throughout a length of about 30 fathoms by a width of about 5½ fathoms and a height of 3 fathoms ; say 500 cubic fathoms for about 500 loads of 45⅔ tons of the ore of the final washing, or about one-half of one per cent. of the weight of the rock. The only vein of magnetite known is at Hatakeyama in Oomaki village, three leagues south of Amegawa ;

but it is only a quarter of a foot thick and is therefore quite unwork able.

The Amegawa iron works are over 100 years old. The only furnace there, like the others of Idzumo, makes both pig iron and steel in one operation of three days; but across the mountains in Bingo with similar furnaces they make, it is said, only pig iron in an operation four days long. The furnace is essentially like the blast furnace of Western countries, but extremely low and with a very long horizontal section and of extremely little durability, as it is built merely of a common yellow clay. The shape is closely like that of the Rachette furnace, a recent invention of Western countries; the size, however, is small. The height is only 3.7 feet, and the width at top 3.2 feet outside or 2.4 feet inside, but the length is 9½ feet outside. The outer sides are battering, and the inner ones still more so near the bottom, so that only half a foot in width along the middle of the bottom is flat. The vertical section crosswise differs then from that of the blast furnace in being widest at the top instead of near the middle. In the course of the operation, however, the inner sides rapidly wear away towards the bottom, so that the section becomes much wider there than at first. The extreme lowness of the furnace can be accounted for by the fact that the minuteness of the particles of the ore enable them to be deoxidized in a very short descent. The great length of the furnace is made up for by a row of nineteen tweers on each side, for which there are elliptical holes 0.2 foot high and 0.7 foot above the bottom outside and 0.5 foot inside; so that the heat is kept up throughout the whole length. The progress of the smelting can also be viewed through the holes at the side of nozzles, and any obstructing slag can be poked away with a small rod inserted there; and at each end of the furnace at the bottom there is a hole 0.4 foot in diameter for drawing off slag and pig iron, and there likewise the smelting can be watched. At the end of the first twenty-four hours that hole is closed and two other similar ones are opened on either side of it near the corners, as the side walls have already become thin. Below the bottom, which is on a level with the ground, there is a layer 0.8 foot thick of ashes of the maki, a conifer (Podocarpus macrophylla); and below them there are 4.2 feet in depth by 3½ feet in width and 9½ feet in length of hot coals; and the five feet together are called the fukutoko, or hearth. Below it is a depth of seven feet filled with red and black clay; from the bottom of which there is a horizontal drain to a neighboring hillside. The whole depth of twelve feet is walled about with half a foot or more in thickness of stone (granite and other kinds). The fukutoko, with the parts below, is permanent, and at some places is not allowed to cool down for a hundred years. The furnace proper is built of wet clay in a day, and dried with a wood fire in the following night.

At three o'clock the next morning the same brands from the wood-fire are removed and the furnace filled with large charcoal, the tweers are adjusted, the coals kindled, and the blast begun. At about five o'clock the charcoal in burning has become about 0.4 of a foot shallower than at first. Then they put on iron sand, perhaps about 16 kamme (133⅓ pounds, or one picul), but not a weighed quantity; then some more charcoal until the top is made level again with the top of the furnace. When the fire has again become about 0.4 foot lower, another picul of iron sand and some more charcoal are put on; and so on repeatedly. The first day and night, ore and charcoal are charged about 33 times in 12 hours; and the second day at about the same rate but growing quicker, so that on the third day there are 42 charges in 12 hours. Throughout the operation, slag is running out at the end-holes of the furnace, and some pig iron, too, called dzuku, which, though variable, amounts to perhaps 180 kamme (1,500 pounds) in all. On the fourth morning at three o'clock (that is, at the end of 72 hours), after having charged in all about 3,800 kamme of charcoal and 3,600 kamme (30,000 pounds) of ore, they stop the blast (which has been continuous) and take away the nozzles. Then they break up the furnace, brush off the coals that remain on the mass of metal that has been produced, and let it cool. The mass is steel, but the outside of it is bad steel called kera; below it there is melted pig iron, or dzuku, which on the removal of the steel mass cools and becomes solid at once. The steel mass weighs about 540 kamme (4,500 pounds), of which two-thirds are good steel and the rest kera. The two are separated with the hammer. The dzuku weighs about 360 kamme (3,000 pounds), or together with the previous 180 kamme (1,500 pounds), about 540 kamme (4,500 pounds) in all; making the whole product then about 1,080 kamme (9,000 pounds or about four tons) or 30 per cent. of the ore. With a larger furnace sometimes 1,200 kamme are produced. When the metal has been cooling a couple of hours, at about six o'clock in the morning the steel mass is pulled out and then immediately the dzuku. The dzuku without further cooling is thrown at once into a small pond of water close by, and is afterwards broken up with hammers. The hot steel mass is likewise thrown into water at some places, but not here; and, after cooling, it is broken up into small bits. The same day that the metal masses are removed the furnace is rebuilt, so that on the fifth day the blowing recommences. In a month, then, there are seven or eight operations, except when occasionally there are interruptions from disordered apparatus. In a year there are about 70 operations with a vacation of two months in the hottest part of summer. The dzuku and kera both go to forges in other villages ; Komuri, two leagues distant ; Komaki, two leagues ; Yakawa, three leagues ; Maki, three leagues ; Sumoni, two leagues, and are converted into bar iron there, yielding about 62½ per cent. [by processes closely similar to those of Western countries, with bloomary and chafery forges]. The dzuku is sometimes made in other villages into good cast iron by means of twice remelting.

The blast is given by a pair of wooden bellows on each side of the furnace, and they are like the bellows of an oil well, except that they are in two halves, end to end, with the hinges on the top boards at the outer ends, so that the man who treads them stands in the middle and steps first on one board and then on the other. The boards are each five feet long by three wide and rise and fall at the inner end about 1½ feet. The work is so severe that the men are relieved about once an hour, and in the twenty-four hours there are three sets of men, or six men in all. The nozzle is chiefly of bamboo, about 0.15 foot in diameter, but at the furnace end is of iron for a length of about two-thirds of a foot, and at the very end with an inside diameter of 0.06 foot. The furnace and bellows, charcoal and ore bins, and resting rooms for the workmen are all in a high building about fifty feet square.

Of wood about 2,000 kamme are used in the three days' operation ; 1,000 kamme for drying the furnace, and 1,000 kamme expressly for making ashes. For the ashes maki only is used ; and it has to be burned green, otherwise, it is said, the ashes are inferior. The ashes would seem to serve as a flux, and at the same time form the bottom of the furnace through which the metal and slag do not penetrate.

The charcoal used is very large, some pieces two or three feet long by half a foot in diameter, but many smaller, and it is broken up a little before putting on the fire. The coals in the fukutoko do not diminish in several years, and when the work is interrupted are kept warm by a mound-shaped charcoal fire on top covered with clay except a hole at one end before which a few sticks of wood burn slowly.

One steel mass (with kera), that I saw, was of irregular shape, about nine feet long by about 3½ feet wide and half a foot thick, including some cinders and ashes on top and slag below, and the dzuku is said to be of about the same shape but much thinner. The kera surrounds the good steel on all sides. The breaking up into small pieces is done partly with hand hammers by eight men, and, in the case of the more difficult lumps, by letting fall upon each of them a mass of dzuku weighing 360 kamme from a height of some ten feet. The mass is raised by means of a rude tread-wheel worked by four men, and falls between a guiding frame-work about 2½ feet square. The twelve men in all do the breaking up in four days, just the time of one complete furnace campaign.

Besides the twelve men who break up the steel (with 48 days' labor) and the six men who blow the furnace (with 18 days' labor), there are two men for charging the charcoal and two for the ore (twelve days' labor) and twelve men for building the furnace (twelve days' labor), so that there are in all ninety days' labor for each operation.

The cost of labor is very low, because strongly attached old family retainers are employed. The bellows' men and steel breakers average about nine cents a day, including four cents worth of rice (one shoo). It is owing to such low wages that the works still succeed no worse. At washing the ore of the hillside near the furnace about ten cents a day are earned. Ore brought from a distance is bought at about 14 cents for a load of 24 kamme. After washing again at the furnace and reduction to one-half its weight, it is worth 25 cents a load (so stated, but the two bought loads to make one of the last washing would cost 28 cents); and the yield therefore is at least 3⅛ cents to the cubic yard of such rock as that near the furnace. Charcoal costs about 12 cents for 10 kamme. Maki wood is worth from 2½ to 3 cents for 10 kamme according to quality. The steel sells for about $5 a load of 30 kamme (or $44.80 a ton), or about $60 for the product of one operation, but averaged say $45. A like load of dzuku and of the best kera (yielding 50 or 60 per cent. of iron) brings about $2 a load (or $17.92 a ton) both alike, or say $48 for the whole product of them in one operation. The making of bar iron from dzuku and kera costs, it is said, about $2.70 a load, but with inferior dzuku and kera it costs more. Bar iron sells at Amegawa for $5 to $7 for 24 kamme according to the quality, averaging, perhaps, $6, or say $67 a ton. Dzuku brings $3 a load (or about $27 a ton) at Matsue.

The chief expenses of the 70 operations of a whole year would be:

266,000 kamme charcoal, ...	$3,192
140,000 kamme wood, say, ...	385
10,500 loads of ore @ 25 sen, ...	2,625
6,300 days' labor @ 9 sen, ...	567
Clay for furnace building say, ...	70
	$6,839

or \$97.90 for each operation, or \$24.34 for each ton of product. But something should be added for the wear and tear of tools and of the breaking machine, deterioration of the buildings, cost of superintendence, and interest on the capital.

The whole product for the same year of 70 operations would be 281 tons (75,600 kamme), of which one-third would be good steel. The value of the whole product would be at say \$93 for each operation, \$6,510 (or at \$108 it would be \$7,560). The information is not quite precise enough to decide with certainty whether there be any profit or not.

The day I visited Amegawa the furnace was not in blast; and the operation is given as it was described to me on the spot. As such inquiries are unusual there and were unexpected, and the answers had not been specially prepared, it is possible there may in some points be a little inexactness, though evidently no more than under the circumstances was unavoidable. It will, therefore, be well to compare the statements with those obtained at the closely similar establishment of Une and with the observations of the operation there.

The Une Iron Works are 103 years old (since 1776); and they say that the fire has in that time never gone out.

The furnace is 9.3 feet by 3.3 feet, as they told me; but by Mr. Adachi's measurement of the patterns, the outside width at the top was 3.4 feet, the inside 2.7 feet; the outside width at the bottom 3.7 feet, and the inside 0.65 foot. There are twenty tweers on each side. The furnace-house, bellows, and other apparatus are closely like those at Amegawa; and my short visit was at about six o'clock in the evening of the second day of the operation. Each bellows was making about 28 strokes a minute with one-half of the bellows, or say 14 strokes for each pair, and the effort was very violent. For the three days eight men are employed to tread the bellows, and on the second day were changing 12 times in the daytime and about 10 times in the night. On the first day the treading is slower and the changing less frequent; on the third day more rapid and more frequent. They change about once for two charges of the furnace, that is, about once an hour. The treading of the two men on the opposite sides of the furnace keeps time, so that the air rushes in from both sides at once, and the flames (about three feet and a half high) rise slightly higher at that instant.

The iron sand is charged only along the sides near the walls of the furnace, and the charcoal is charged slightly nearer the middle. When freshly charged the charcoal rises slightly (about a quarter of a foot) above the top of the furnace. At the time of my visit they were charging three times an hour, and on the third day they charge still oftener.

The ore charged in one operation of three days amounts to 220 or 230 boxes of 14 or 15 kamme (sometimes 17 or 18 kamme), say 3,300 kamme (but possibly about 3,600 kamme, as at Amegawa). Of charcoal, in the same time, 4,200 or 4,300 kamme are charged; and of wood, 720 or 730 kamme are used for making ashes, and 1,200 or 1,300 kamme for drying the furnace, about 2,000 kamme in all. The ashes have to be made for each operation.

The clay for building the furnace has to be brought from a distance of three-quarters of a mile (11 choo), from land belonging to the furnace owner, and the carriage costs $0.0043 for ten kamme and the digging somewhat more; say in all about one dollar for the 800 or 1,000 kamme that are needed for a furnace.

There is always some slag with the dzuku at the end of the operation below the level of the bottom of the furnace, the ashes and coals beneath having become somewhat depressed, but it does not penetrate the ashes.

The whole product of one operation is from 720 to 1,020 kamme (6,000 to 8,500 pounds), or about 30 per cent., as at Amegawa, sometimes 1,200 kamme (10,000 pounds); of which the dzuku varies from 90 to 480 kamme (750 to 4,000 pounds). There are about sixty operations in a year, but the number varies in different years. They are idle in July and August, and in 1878 began blowing on the seventh of September. They say that in the hot weather the metal does not melt so well as it does in the cold, probably the labor of treading the bellows so rapidly is too severe in hot weather; but the draft upward from the fire would be slightly less active and the air slightly rarer.

In Bingo, where with a four days' operation dzuku alone is made, the furnace is said to be longer and narrower, about 10 feet by 2.8 feet. If the furnace is narrow there is less charcoal, and so not enough heat for steel, they say; but for dzuku alone less charcoal is needed. The tweers are about 20 (18 to 21) on each side of the furnace and are a little smaller than for making steel. The dzuku is drawn off in a melted state by the holes at the end of the furnace. In other respects, they say, the Bingo process does not specially differ from the Idzumo one.

As the Japanese method of making pig iron from sand ore is the only one successfully practiced in any part of the world, and as the amount of such ore in Japan seems to be very large indeed, it is worth while to consider whether the process cannot be so improved as to be more decidedly profitable. The whole cost of the steel and pig iron product appears to be made up mainly in the following proportions :

```
Charcoal, . . . . . . . . . . .46⅔ per cent.
Ore, . . . . . . . . . . . . .38⅓   "    "
Labor :
    Breaking,  . . . . . 4½        "    "
    Blowing, . . . . . . 1½        "    "
    Charging,  . . . . . 1  .      "    "
                         —— 7      "    "
Furnace :
    Wood for drying,  . . 4
    Clay, . . . . . . . 1
    Labor, . . . . . . . 1
                         —— 6      "    "
Wood for ashes, . . . . .     2    "    "
                         ——
                         100
```

Evidently the cost of fuel and ore are far the most important items. It must be borne in mind, however, that nearly all the remaining fifteen per cent. are only about half-price, owing to the exceptionally low wages paid at the iron works. It seems clear that much economy might be effected as regards: 1st, washing of the ore ; 2d, the carrying of the ore, fuel, and other materials ; 3d, the fuel ; 4th, the flux ; 5th, the breaking of the metal ; 6th, the blast ; 7th, the furnace building.

APPENDIX B TO THE PAPER ON JAPANESE SWORDS.

SHAKUDÔ.

From the *Wakansansaidzue*, Vol. 59, fol. 15.

Shakudô has a purplish black color.   Shakudô is written with characters that mean red copper; but whence comes the character red is not clear.   The mode of preparation is as follows : To 100 momme in weight of copper add 30 momme of shirome [" the best quality of tin," but the same word is now used for antimony], and melt ; the product is called nikurome. To 100 momme of the nikurome add 4 sen [*i. e.,* apparently 4 momme] of gold, and melt.   Then steep the product in four half pounds [or one quart] of vinegar with four momme of rokushô [blue vitriol] and one shoo [nearly two quarts] of water, and the black color appears.

Imitations are made with merely copper steeped as above mentioned ; or by exposing it to sulphur smoke.

President Brinton spoke as follows, on

"INSCRIPTIONS FROM EASTER ISLAND."

"Easter Island," he said, "presents a curious phenomenon. It is 2,100 miles from the coast of South America, and 1,000 miles from the nearest inhabited land, Pitcairn Island. Discovered about 1680, its inhabitants were found in possession of a civilization in advance of that of neighboring islands. A most curious feature was large statues that were found upon platforms overlooking the ocean. The number of these is not yet estimated. The largest, according to Surgeon George H. Cooke, U. S. N., is an unfinished obelisk, 69 feet 9 inches in height. The art of the rudiments of writing was understood by the inhabitants, an art not understood by the people of any of the other islands."

Copies of the inscriptions were then exhibited. "These," Dr. Brinton said, "were usually cut into wooden slabs, with sharp fragments of obsidian, and were also painted upon the walls of their houses and temples. They were used for various purposes : to record genealogies, to send messages, and as ornaments on shields. Information was sent, by means of them, from one part of the island to another, but a knowledge of the writing was confined to a very limited class—the kings and the priests. The German steamer ' Hyäne' visited the island in 1883, and found the message-sticks still in use and understood by an old chief, Hangeto. The general character of the writing is illustrated by a genealogical scroll, made some years ago by one of the Spanish visitors, a copy of which I exhibit. Most of the writings are genealogical tablets.

"The art was confined with them to picture or symbol-writing. Each picture conveys a definite idea, and the pictures were usually of objects most familiar in fact or theory, as certain mythical animals they believe in, or certain of their gods. Those relating to the sexual relation are the most prominent. Their principal god is *Máke-Máke*, a bi-sexual divinity represented by a figure of two sea-birds. Their principal weapon of war is in the form of a paddle, which terminates in a phallus.

"The name of the island is differently interpreted. Surgeon Cooke, who visited the island in 1886, gives the name by which it is known to the natives as *Tepíta te Henúa*, ' the navel and the womb,' and *Rapa nui* as the name given to it by the Tahitians. *Rapa nui* is said to be the proper name. The island has an area of 34 square miles. Thirty years ago it had 3,000, but now it has only 155 inhabitants. According to the first account, it had 20,000 people, but this number is probably exaggerated. The statues on the sea-coast are all very much alike. They are not ancestral, and not all phallic. Each has an appropriate name. According to Captain Geiseler, of the 'Hyäne,' they are all of native Polynesian construction.''

MAY 1ST.

Mr. Culin spoke at length with reference to the Society's pressing need of a more suitable hall for its meetings, and a discussion of the subject followed.

MAY 12TH.

A special meeting was held this evening, at the written request of seven members, to consider the question of purchasing a house for the Society.

Mr. Thomas Hockley, of the Committee appointed March 6th, stated that the Committee had examined a number of properties, among which the most desirable was the house at the southeast corner of Twenty-first and Pine Streets.

MAY 17TH.

A special meeting of the Society was held this afternoon, at No. 205 South Sixth Street.

The Committee appointed to secure better accommodations for the Society reported, through its Chairman, Mr. Jordan, that it advised that authority be given to it to purchase the house at the southeast corner of Twenty-first and Pine Streets. This report was accepted, and its recommendations authorized.

JUNE 9TH.

A special meeting of the Society was held this afternoon, at No. 205 South Sixth Street, at which it was reported that the purchase of the house at the southeast corner of Twenty-first and Pine Streets had been consummated, and the following Committee was appointed to solicit contributions, to be applied to paying off the indebtedness: Francis Jordan, Jr., Thomas Hockley, Carl Edhelheim, Cornelius Stevenson, and Stewart Culin. The following Building Committee was also appointed: Thomas Hockley, Francis Jordan, Jr., and Cornelius Stevenson.

JUNE 26TH.

A special meeting of the Society was held this afternoon, at No. 205 South Sixth Street. Mr. Wilson Eyre exhibited plans he had made, at the request of the Building Committee, for a new building for the Society, upon the site of the existing building at the southeast corner of Twenty-first and Pine Streets.

OCTOBER 2D.

It was concluded to defer the permanent improvement of the property recently purchased by the Society, and the Building Committee was authorized to have necessary alterations made to the existing building.

NOVEMBER 6TH.

The stated meeting was held this evening at the house of the President, Dr. Daniel G. Brinton, No. 2041 Chestnut Street. President Brinton delivered an account of the recent Congress of Americanists in Paris, in which, after dwelling upon the most striking features of the Congress, he referred to the entire forgetfulness of national antagonisms as one of its most gratifying features, and spoke of the important aid rendered by science in doing away with such enmities and bringing about harmonious relations between all peoples.

DECEMBER 4TH.

The stated meeting was again held at the house of President Brinton.

Dr. Robert H. Lamborn exhibited two silver coins of the short-lived kingdom of Etruria, which are said to be among the finest examples of modern coinage.

Mr. Culin exhibited a number of Roman coins of Marcus Aurelius, Domitian, and Antoninus Pius, found in the well of St. Albans, near Roanne, in the Bourbonnais, France, where they had been thrown as votive offerings.

President Brinton exhibited two stones resembling stone axes, which had been picked up on Rye Beach, N. H. One of them resembled a small stone axe so closely that it was difficult to say whether it was the work of man or the result of natural forces. The groove followed a soft striation in the stone and was slightly sloping, from which it was concluded by the members present that it was a natural formation.

President Brinton, in commenting upon the paper read by Prof. Frederick Starr at the recent meeting of the American Folk-Lore Society in New York City on the Folk-lore of Stone Implements, stated that in New Jersey the belemnite, a fossil found in the marl, was there known as " thunder stone," the term by which stone axes are so generally known. President Brinton exhibited a collection of objects consisting of flint chips, an argillite implement of very pure shape, and some pieces of pottery from Peter's Island in the Schuylkill River. Dr. Brinton also exhibited a manuscript copy of the first book of Sahagun's *History of Mexico* from the original MSS. in the Medicean library in Florence. This precious object, the existence of which was first publicly made known by Dr. Brinton, was compiled by Sahagun from the original Aztec records. It consists of twelve books, written in Nahuatl, with a Spanish translation. The latter is very free and much abbreviated. It is illustrated with no less than 1,300 pictures, colored in the symbolic manner peculiar to the ancient Mexicans. The volume exhibited consisted of the Nahuatl text of the first volume, which treats of the Mexican gods, with copies in color of the original pictures made by a skillful artist in Florence, under the direction of the present owners. The original remains unpublished, and this is the first and only copy ever made.

In a discussion that followed the exhibition of this work, the opinion was expressed that no more important contribution could be made to any of our libraries in the interest of students of American antiquities than the reproduction of the remaining volume of this work. An offer to defray one-third of the expense of such a reproduction was made. A valuable collection of coins, comprising the most important addition to its cabinet received in recent years, was presented to the Society by Francis C. Macauley, Esq. This collection, numbering 1,385 specimens, comprised a large number of Roman coins, notable for their perfect condition, some interesting specimens of mediæval coinage, modern European and Oriental silver and gold pieces, and a quantity of American silver, much of the latter being proofs. A special vote of thanks was tendered to Mr. Macauley for his gift.

1891.

JANUARY 8TH.

The first meeting of the Society in its new Hall, southeast corner
of Twenty-first and Pine Streets, was held this evening with President
Brinton in the chair. Mr. Francis C. Macauley presented a French
gold coin, which was comprised in a treasure found in tearing down an
old building on the site now occupied by the banking house of the
Crédit Lyonnais in Paris.

FEBRUARY 5TH.

Mr. Culin read the following paper, entitled

"EAST INDIAN FORTUNE-TELLING WITH DICE."

There is a popular notion that the East, especially India and China,
is still the repository of many valuable arts and sciences that are unknown in Europe. Indeed, there is a widely-spread belief that if we
could but penetrate its mysteries, Asia would reveal to us rich treas-
ures of knowledge, wherein we should find anticipated many of the
discoveries of modern science.

It is hinted even by some of the more scholarly that traces of a secret
learning, embodying higher conceptions of the universe and its phenomena than those with which we are acquainted, are to be found in
the ancient philosophies and religions of the Orient, and stories are
frequently related of the apparently supernatural control which Indian
adepts obtain over the forces of nature by means of their extraordinary
and mysterious knowledge.

It is not for me to assert that Asia has not its lore, and lore, too, of
which we know absolutely nothing ; for I am assured it has sciences
and philosophies and secret doctrines of which we do not even know
the names, and which, no doubt, will be lost and perish utterly, without attracting more than a passing glance from Western scholars. But
I am skeptical as to their value, save as illustrating the possible vaga-

5

65

ries of the human mind, and regard the notions about the learning of the East as a popular delusion, so far as that learning is supposed to transcend the deductions of Western scholars. It is to a few pages, however, from the occult lore of the East, of India, the treasure-house of mystery, that I intend to turn, and present to you an account of the methods of divination with dice as there existing at the present day. Whatever may be its interest, and serious value I can hardly claim for it, the subject has at least the advantage of novelty, for I hazard little in saying that until the present moment its secrets have never been revealed for criticism and discussion by Occidental scholars.

The custom of telling fortunes with dice is universal throughout India, where it is regarded as a science under the name of *ramala*, and is practiced as means of livelihood by a large number of persons who are called *ramali*. The science, so-called, is popularly believed to be of great antiquity, and is said to have been founded about 6,000 years ago by *Garga*, who wrote many treatises on *jyotis*, "astronomy," as well as on the subject of *ramala*. To him is attributed the authorship of the work entitled *Prasna-manorama*, to which further reference will be made.

The literature of *ramala* is very extensive, and, according to Swami Bhaskara Nand Saraswati, to whom I am indebted for the information contained in this paper, amounts to over 2,000 works, comprising over 100 different systems.

In early times, he says, *ramala* was not much resorted to, and its great popularity dates from the Mohammedan conquest. It is now current alike among Hindus and Mohammedans. The Hindus use dice made of sandal-wood; the Mohammedans prefer those of metal, combining silver, gold, zinc, iron, brass, copper, and mercury into an alloy for the purpose. The Hindu fortune-tellers pray to Çiva and the Mohammedans to Azrael. Among the Hindus, a person who tells fortunes is called a *jyotiei* and among the Mohammedans a *ramala*.

The dice used in telling fortunes are called *ramala-pâsa*, and differ from the *pâsa* or dice used in playing games, and also vary in shape and marks, according to the system in which they are employed. In all of the systems, so far as I have been able to ascertain, the general procedure is much the same. The inquirer throws the die or dice once or oftener, and the number representing the throw or the sum or multiple of the throws is referred to a book, in which, under a corresponding number, an answer is found. These books were formerly treasured by the *ramali*, who kept them to themselves. Within recent years they have become accessible to every one through printed copies, several of which, illustrating different ways of telling fortunes, were placed in my hands by Mr. Nand.

One of them is entitled *Prasna-manorama* and bears a Calcutta imprint of 1880. Its authorship is said to be disputed, some attributing it to *Garga*, and others to *Parāçara*, who also lived, according to current Indian tradition, about six thousand years ago.

Before proceeding to describe the method of employing it, a few words might be said as to the mode of procedure on visiting a fortune-teller. It is customary to go to him early in the morning. The visitor having requested his services and put, we will say, four pice in his book, the *ramali* prays to Çiva, and entreats the god to come hear and aid him with his power. The *ramali* then requests the inquirer to name one of his hands "gold," we will say, and the other, "silver," and throw the dice. He will thereupon endeavor to tell him which he named "gold," and which "silver." Or he will ask him to think of the name of a flower, as "rose" or "lily," and in the same way, ostensibly from the numbers thrown, informs him which particular flower he thought of. The Swami asserts that the fortune-teller is usually successful, and, in point of fact, he himself succeeded in experiments made with the writer. These preliminaries serve to impress the inquirer, and inspire him with confidence. The dice used in connection with the *Prasna-manorama* are three in number, and consist of square prisms of sandal-wood, about three inches in length, marked with dots, from 3 to 6, on the sides. The *ramali* gives them to the inquirer, and enjoins him to pray seven times to Çiva, and throw the *pāsā*, which are rolled on the palm of the right hand outward from the thrower. The *ramali* notes the sum of the faces of the three dice, and, the operation being performed three times, and three numbers obtained, he refers to the text under these numbers in his book, for an answer to the question that was propounded. This question was not supposed to have been known to the *ramali*, but the inquirer is expected to keep it in mind when he throws the dice. This method my informant regarded as superstitious, but the following one, in which the *Prasna-manorama* is also used, he considered more certain. Indeed, he related that once, when expecting a letter, he went in a spirit of fun to a *ramali*, who told him his letter would arrive in three days, at 11 o'clock, and on the very day and hour, as predicted, he received the letter. Çiva is appealed to, and the three *pāsā* thrown, as before. The *ramali* adds the numbers on the two dice farthest from the thrower, and multiplies their sum by the one nearest the thrower. This is performed three times, and the book consulted each time, as before.

The sum of the three results is then taken and compared with the corresponding numbers in the book. Thus, if the three throws are 6, 6, 4 ; 6, 5, 4, and 4, 6, 4, the calculation may be represented as follows :

$$(6 + 6) \times 4 = 48$$
$$(6 + 5) \times 4 = 44$$
$$(4 + 6) \times 4 = 40$$
$$48 + 44 + 40 = 132$$

and the significant numbers will be found in the columns on the right.

There is still another way of telling fortunes by means of the *Prasna-manorama*. According to this method, the number 438, which represents sums of the numerical values which the fortune-teller attributed to certain letters of the Arabic alphabet, is multiplied by the total of the first throw with three dice ; the second throw subtracted from this result, and the remainder divided by the third throw. The quotient will be the number under which the correct answer should be found in the book, and the remainder will be a significant number, and indicate a number of days, weeks, months, or years, or whatever numerical term is expected in answer to the question. The answers in the book are direct in their character, and are preceded by a question which should be the one asked by the inquirer. Thus, under 440 : "You ask me how many days before you will make a large sum of money. The dice answer that you will not make money very soon." The answers do not always fit the question originally propounded. According to the fortune-tellers, the questions asked by the world are of three kinds, concerning :

> *dhātu*, meaning "money."
> *jiva*, meaning "life."
> *mūla*, meaning "land."

If the seeker into the future does not appear to be satisfied, the *ramali* may verify his answer by adding the last remainder to the quotient and referring the sum to the book. If the answer given under that number is of the same kind as that under the first one, the *ramali* is assured that he has answered the question propounded. He may still further confirm his reply by having the inquirer throw the dice once more, and if the answer in the first part of the *Prasna-mano-rama*, corresponding with the throw, is of the same kind as the original answer, the latter must refer to the subject under consideration. If it is of a different kind, the fortune-teller makes another effort.

Another treatise, entitled *Vitidarpana*, or the "Mirror of Conduct," is said to have been written by Sridhara, whose name means "luck-carrier." It was translated into Hindustani from the Sanskrit about twenty years ago. The copy shown to me was printed at Agra in 1881. One die is used with it, consisting of a square prism of red sandal-wood marked on its sides with the Sanskrit numerals from 1 to 4. In using it the *ramali* prays to Çiva, and requests the inquirer to throw the die three times and keep his question in mind.

The *ramali* writes down the number of each throw, putting the first in the hundreds' place, the second in the tens' place, and the third in the units' place, so that the three throws may be read as a number composed of these elements. Thus, if the throws are 2, 1, 2, he reads them as 212, and refers to the corresponding number in the book. In this system affirmations are used, which are equivalent to questions, and must be approved or negatived by the inquirer, such as "You have received a letter within three or four days?" "The person who wrote the letter lives within 100 miles?" The *ramali* looks under the number, as 212, and proceeds according to the book, which provides for both affirmative and negative answers, until he has asked 12 questions, when the 12th question or affirmation is regarded as an answer to the question propounded.

There is yet another method in which an entirely different kind of dice are used. It is set forth in a work entitled *Parisapaksi*, which is said to have been written by Çiva. The copy shown to me was in Sanskrit, in three large octavo volumes, printed in Calcutta in 1883. This book is divided into chapters, each treating of a different subject, for which the method of procedure is described. Some of the subjects of inquiry are as follows:

The number of years a person will live.
The age of a person.
The number of times ill.
The number of times in danger.
Whether a person has traveled.
The number of his brothers and sisters.
Whether his parents are living.
What he ate to-day.
What he did to-day.
The name of the flower that is thought of, and so on.

The dice employed in this system are eight in number, and are strung, so as to rotate easily, on two metal rods, four on each. The rod passes through the centre of two unmarked sides, the other four sides of each die being dotted from 2 to 4. The set here exhibited are ivory, and were made for the writer in Lucknow. They agree in arrangement and marks with two sets of metal dice, presumably Oriental, in the Sommerville Collection in the Museum of the University of Pennsylvania.

As an illustration of this system I shall give two examples of its employment by Mr. Nand in answering questions propounded by the writer. The first question was, "How long shall I live?" I threw the dice, tossing them outward on the palm as before, and the sum of their upturned faces was 25. He referred to the book and said: "When you were 12 years old you were in danger from water. It was near your birthday, and two boys were with you. You were swimming and your companions saved you. One of the boys lived near to you—next door to your home. The other boy lived farther away. One of them was your schoolmate. The same boy gave you a pearl knife."

At his request I threw the dice again. The result was 21. He

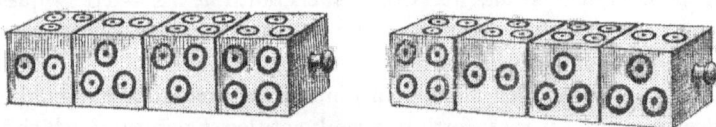

referred to his book, and said, "Between your nineteenth and twentieth years you were sick for two weeks—not very sick."

I threw the dice again. Their sum was 23. He said, "Between your twenty-first and twenty-second year, one of your friends died."

At his request I again threw the dice. By this throw, he said, he would answer my question. One of the sets came up 12, and the other the same. Taking the sum of the two sets ($12 + 12 = 24$) he asked my age, thirty-one years, which he added to the result ($24 + 31 = 55$). He then asked me to think of a number, whatever number I would. I suggested 300. He thereupon added 27 to the last result ($55 + 27 = 82$) and divided 27 by 5, and subtracted the quotient and remainder from the last addition ($27 \div 5 = 5$, with 2 remaining; $82 - 5 = 77$; $77 - 2 = 75$). The result, 75, he declared to be the number of the years of my life. He afterward informed me that 27 was always added when the person was asked to think of a number, no matter what their guess might be, unless they chose a number less than 27, when that lesser number was substituted. The number divided by 5 was in the same way always 27, unless the person chose a number less than 27 ; 5, he explained, was used as a divisor, from the five fingers of the hand.

To find the months, the quotient obtained by dividing the selected number, that is, 27 or less, by 5, should be multiplied by the number of months from the inquirer's last birthday. The result should be divided by the face of the set of dice nearest to the thrower, and the remainder plus the number of months from the last birthday, minus the quotient obtained by dividing, will give the odd months of the inquirer's life. The days are obtained by a similar process, but with less precision, says my informant, than the months and years.

The process of telling the name of a flower that is thought of, according to one of the methods laid down in the *Parisapaksi*, is more intricate than the preceding. I shall merely describe the operation of divining the first letter of the flower's name, when the fortune-teller is assisted by being told the number of letters in its name.

The two sets of dice are thrown three times. The sum of the first throw, say 24, is taken, and that of the faces of the four dice nearest the inquirer on the second throw, say 14, is subtracted from it $(24 - 14 = 10)$. The sum of the third throw, say 25, is added to the last result $(10 + 25 = 35)$, and that of the faces of the dice nearest the inquirer on the second throw, 14, again subtracted $(35 - 14 = 21)$. The number of letters in the flower's name (in the experiment here referred to, the rose) must be subtracted from the last remainder $(21 - 4 = 17)$, and the first figure of the first remainder, 1, added to the result $(17 + 1 = 18)$. The number thus obtained will represent the numerical place in the alphabet, numbered from A downward, of the initial of the flower.

The dice last referred to are the kind that are now generally used throughout India for telling fortunes.

At the conclusion of the paper Mr. Nand, of Jodhpur, India, who was present at the meeting, gave a practical illustration of the methods of telling fortunes described in Mr. Culin's address.

In commenting upon the subject, President Brinton stated that among fortune-tellers here, their predictions seldom relate to life and death, although they frequently refer to money. Questions of love and marriage are here the principal ones.

President Brinton read a letter from Prof. J. C. Branner, State Geologist of Arkansas, in which was inclosed a copy of an inscription on the bluff at Millstone Creek, Ark. (Sec. 25, 13 N., 29 W.). This Dr. Brinton unhesitatingly pronounced a forgery, stating that the writing was of a not unfamiliar form, as he had seen it on many frauds from the West. These fraudulent inscriptions, he stated, usually contain characters that resemble those in the alphabets contained on one of the pages in the back part of Webster's Unabridged Dictionary, and this, he suggested, probably furnished an inspiration to the makers of such deceptions.

Mr. Culin exhibited a board for *dama*, drafts, and *taula* (our backgammon), with a pair of dice, from Damascus, which had recently been obtained by him for the collection of objects used in games in the Museum of the University of Pennsylvania. The board, which was said to be over 100 years old, was inlaid with silver wire, ivory, and mother of pearl.

APRIL 2D.

Mrs. Cornelius Stevenson, Honorary Curator of the Egyptian Department of the Museum of Archæology and Palæontology of the University of Pennsylvania, who had been invited to address the Society, read the following paper:

ON CERTAIN SYMBOLS USED IN THE DECORATION OF SOME POTSHERDS FROM DAPHNÆ AND NAUKRATIS,

NOW IN THE MUSEUM OF THE UNIVERSITY OF PENNSYLVANIA.

The painted potsherds to which I would call attention, belong to the collection recently sent to the Museum of the University of Pennsylvania by the "Egypt Exploration Fund," and form a part of the discoveries made by Mr. William M. Flinders-Petrie, on the ancient sites of Daphnæ and Naukratis in the Delta.

The geographical position of these sites, and the period of history to which they belong—*i.e.*, a period full of commercial activity, and of brisk intercourse between the Mediterranean peoples and the civilized nations of Western Asia and Northern Africa, who one and all contributed their share to the development of Greek thought, make these potsherds particularly valuable for the purpose of tracing the gradual evolution of certain artistic forms which have become familiar in decorative art. And the fact that those in charge of the excavations, keenly appreciating the requirements of modern science, spared no pains to establish the historical stratum and the exact surroundings of every fragment discovered by them, has added the greatest possible value to the "finds." Moreover, by means of the published reports of the explorers, we not only possess all the necessary data concerning the specimens obtained by us, but we are able to trace the companion sherds which have found their way into other museums, so that, although our own series may be incomplete, we often can, for the purpose of study, supply its deficiencies by means of the published plates.[1]

The Human-Headed Bird.

For instance, among the number of smaller pieces sent to the Museum of the University are two fragments of a vase of red-glaze incised

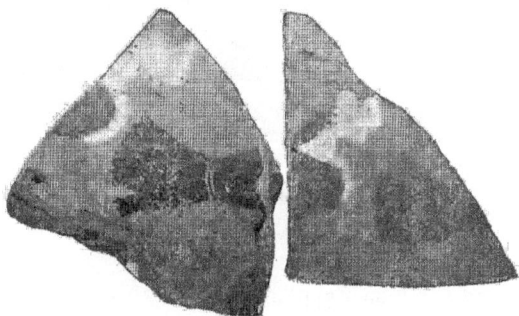

Fig. 19. Potsherd from Daphnæ. Mus. of the University of Pennsylvania.

painted ware (fig. 19), found at Tel-Defenneh—(N. E. Delta), which upon referring to plate xxxi, fig. 4, of Mr. Petrie's work upon that site, may be seen to represent the head and tail of the human-headed bird later known in Greek art as a Harpy (fig. 20). [The wings and middle portion of the body are missing in our specimen, although

Fig. 20. Potsherd from Daphnæ, W. M. Flinders-Petrie, *Tanis* II, pl. xxxi, fig. 4.

sufficient trace of the former remains to indicate that, in their form, they were similar to those in the published specimens, in which the head is wanting. Comparing the two, we have the complete bird.]

It is worthy of remark that a variation of this form is found on a fine Œnochoé from Kamiros (Rhodes), in the British Museum. The

[1] See *Tanis*, Part II, *Nebesheh* (Am.) and *Defenneh* (Tapahnes) by Mr. W. M. Flinders-Petrie. Also, *Naukratis*, Parts I and II.

attitude and the body and tail are very similar to those in our example, but the wings are spread out instead of being held up erect.[1]

Fig. 21. Egyptian Soul-Bird.

The older and common Egyptian form of this fanciful creation is herewith given (fig. 21). Thus it was that the Egyptians portrayed the soul which they call "Baï." It is sometimes depicted with out-

Fig. 22. From Sir G. Wilkinson's *Manners and Customs of the Ancient Egyptians*, III, p. 158.

stretched wings, fluttering over the mummy, holding in its hand the emblem of life—*i. e.*, the Cross—or presenting to it both the Cross

[1] A. S. Murray, *Handbook of Greek Archæology*, p. 62.

and the Sail, which was the hieroglyph for breath[1] (fig. 22). Another form shows it standing by the side of a coffin, with raised hands, in an attitude of invocation.[2] Another still (fig. 23), under the sycamore tree, receiving from the mother-goddess the waters of life.[3]

Fig. 23. From Sir G. Wilkinson's *Manners and Customs of the Ancient Egyptians*, III, p. 64.

Among people of primitive culture, the notion that birds are transformed disembodied spirits seems to be a common one. Night birds, such as bats and owls, who haunt caves and are found living where the remains of the dead have been deposited, are particularly so regarded.[4] Many examples might be furnished of such ideas being prevalent not only among modern races in a low stage of intellectual development,[5] but among the nations of antiquity.

[1] Wilkinson's *Manners and Customs of the Ancient Egyptians*, Vol. III, p. 158. New Ed.

[2] *Gazette des Beaux Arts*. Reproduced by E. Soldi in *Les Arts Méconnus*, p. 488.

[3] *Wilkinson, loc. cit.*, III, pp. 64 and 119.

[4] H. Spencer, *Principles of Sociology*, 1865, p. 329.

[5] Among the indigenous races of America the notion that associates night birds with

The Rig Veda (I, 165, 4) directs the worshipper to curse death and
the God of the dead, when the owl emits her dismal cry; and this

death, and sees even in ordinary birds, spirits of the departed, is a very general one.
The owl was regarded by the Aztecs, the Quichés, the Mayas, the Peruvians, the
Araucanians, and the Algonquins as sacred to the Lord of Death, whose messenger it
was. (D. G. Brinton's *Myths of the New World*, p. 106. Among the Quichés, not
only were owls looked upon as departed spirits, but they were supposed to take part
in the affairs of men. (*Ibid.*, p. 64.)

The Dakota children have a " Ghost-game " which betrays the light in which the
owl is regarded among their people. One of them erects a hut outside the village,
and at night comes hooting like an owl and scratching on the outside of the tent.
(J. Owen Dorsey, *Am. Anthrop.*, October 1st, 1891, p. 330.)

The Aztecs thought that the spirits of all good people as a reward became embodied in birds, and the Powhatans believed that the souls of princes passed into birds.
(D. G. Brinton's *loc. cit.*, p. 102.)

In Iroquois mythology a small bird (Saxonis fusca) is supposed to have come from
a human pair changed by the Creator, who doomed them to inhabit caves, ruins, and
such places. (J. N. B. Hewitt, *Am. Anthrop.*, January 1st, 1892, p. 36.) Moreover,
when a man died they set off a bird who was supposed to carry off with it the spirit
of the dead. (Schoolcraft, 113 ; Comp. E. B. Tylor, *Prim. Cult.*, II, 9.

In Tierra del Fuego the souls of the dead are supposed to enter the bodies of
ducks, and after some English travelers had been out duck-shooting, the natives tried
to placate the spirits by blowing. (A. Réville, *Religions des Peuples non civilisés*,
II, p. 399.)

The Abipones also think that the soul flies off under the shape of a duck. (*Ibid.*,
I, 386.)

The Hurons and the Mandans looked upon doves as spirits of the departed. (D.
G. Brinton, *loc. cit.*, p. 107, quoting *Rela. de la Nelle. France, An.*, 1636, Chap. IX),
and acc. to Coreal *Voy. aux Indes Occ.* II, p. 132, quoted also by D. G. Brinton,
loc. cit., p. 254.) The inhabitants of Popoyan would not kill doves because they
believed them to be animated by the souls of the departed.

Similar ideas are found in other parts of the world. For instance, the Orang Kou-
bous of Sumatra, believe that the departed spirit flies above the soul where the body
rests (*Bulletin de la Soc. d'Anthrop.*, Jan., Feb., 1891, p. 32), and in the
Philippines bats are treated with respect by the natives for similar reasons. (See
H. Spencer, *Principles of Sociology*, 1885, p. 330.) The same author quoting
M. Caussin de Perceval says that the Arabs believed that " when the soul left the
body it flew away in the form of a bird which they called Hâma or Sada (a sort of
owl), and did not cease flying around the tomb crying pitifully."

Mr. Codrington, *Journ. of the Anthrop. Inst.* X, 261, tells of a woman from the
Banks Islands who, knowing a neighbor at the point of death, heard a fluttering
in her house just as the cries outside showed her that the man had died. She
caught the flying creature and ran with it to her neighbor's, crying that she had caught
the " atai" (spirit, personality) and opened her hand over the corpse's mouth, of course
with no result. Other similar beliefs exist among the Samoans. (See H. Spencer,
loc. cit., p. 796.)

To this day in the folk lore of France relating to the legends connected with the
night-hunt, the Souls of the Dead are often alluded to as doves who, pursued by

bird was brought into close relation by the Hindus with the God
Yama who ruled the underworld. The crow was also closely connected by them with the shades of the departed, and when funereal
offerings were given to the crows, souls were supposed to pass into a
better world.[1]

In the Odyssey [2] the spirits of the dead are said to "twitter like
bats and scream like frightened birds," and the Hebrew soothsayers,
when consulting the shades of departed ancestors, are represented by
Isaiah as chirping like birds.[3]

A survival of the idea may be detected in the widespread, unreason-
ing and superstitious dread inspired by bats, and even owls, among cultivated people of our own day. Indeed, I have known the feeling to
be extended to the accidental visit of ordinary birds by some persons
who look upon such an occurrence as an omen of death. And the
numerous legends connected with vampires have a similar origin in the
past.

In the Chaldæan story of Ishtar, she is represented as threatening
that, unless she be admitted to the realm of the dead, she will let them
out to devour the living.[4] But although the ancient Babylonians conceived the soul after death as "clad like birds in a garment of feath-

---

Satan, only find rest under the protection of the Cross. (See *Les Acousmates et les
Chasses fantastiques*, by E. Henry Carnoy, *Rev. de l' Histoire des Relig.*, IX, 375.)

In the *Chron. of the Beatified Anthony*, quoted by Gubernatis (*Zoological
Mythol.*, II, 254), fetid black pools are described in *Regione puteolorum in Apulia*,
whence the souls arise in the forms of monstrous birds, in the evening hours of the
Sabbath, and wander till, in the morning, an enormous crow compels them to submerge
themselves and to disappear.

In Hungary, as indeed in many other countries, the owl is the bird of death and its
cry a bad omen. (Comp. Gubernatis *loc. cit.*, where many such superstitions are
mentioned as existing among Aryan peoples.)

[1] Gubernatis, *Zoological Mythol.*, II, 254.

[2] *Odyssey*, xxiv, 5–10.

[3] *Isaiah* viii, 9. "And when they say unto you inquire of the spirits" (the word is
based upon the meaning of ancestors) "and of the soothsayers" (literally : those who
know) "who chirp and who murmur—should not a nation inquire of its God through
the living, the dead?" I am indebted to Dr. Morris Jastrow for the above analysis
of this interesting passage.

Among the Polynesians there is a widespread notion that ghosts have a chirping,
whistling voice. In the Tonga Islands it was forbidden to whistle because it was tantamount to imitating the voice of the gods. (Albert Réville, *loc. cit.*, II, 96.)

[4] Sayce, *Hibbert Lectures*, page 146, says "under the shape of vampires." Ménant,
Recherches sur la glyptique orientale, p. 177, says under the shape "of wolves."
It is curious to find this passage giving rise to these two interpretations—when, as a
matter of fact, the notion which inspired it has given birth to the two conceptions of

ers;"[1] or "Like birds clothed with wings,"[2] I am unaware of their having originally used this form to illustrate the notion in art.[3] It is in Egypt that we first find the soul-bird represented in a visible shape, and we may therefore consider the Nile Valley to be its birthplace as an artistic form.

the "vampire" and the "Loup-garou" or were-wolf, both weird embodiments of the disincarnate human spirit, regarded as preying upon the living.

The Keres of death, who, in Greek mythology, "stretch men in the grave" (*Iliad*, viii, 70) and whom Hesiod shows us flying over the battle-field "gnashing their white teeth," terrible, insatiable, struggling for the fallen warriors, " thirsting for their black blood," who, when they he'd a wounded warrior, buried their talons into his flesh " and sent his soul into Hades—in the Chilly Tartarus "—seem as though they might be actors of the scene of violence threatened by the great Chaldean nature-goddess. " See Hesiod, *The Shield of Herakles*, 249." And the notion of the souls of the dead thirsting for blood appears in the Odyssey, when the blood of Ulysses' sacrifice draws the phantoms of the dead "like flies."

[1] " Descent of Ishtar into Hades " f. 10.   Sayce, *The Relig. of the Ancient Babyl.*, *Hibbert Lect.*, 1887, 221.

[2] G. Smith, *Assyr. Disc.*, p. 203, Legend of Isdubar.

[3] The extraordinary scene from Tello now in the Louvre, where birds of prey are depicted bearing away the limbs of the dead on a battle-field—is obviously a scene of carnage symbolical of victory.   (See Léon Heuzey, *Les origines orientales*, p. 40, etc. Comp. with M. de Sarzec, *Découvertes en Chaldée*, pl. i, 2–3.)

The nearest approach to the artistic form of the human-headed bird which I have been able to find among the antiquities of Mesopotamia is on a remarkable cylinder of lapis-lazuli in the museum of the Hague—published by M. Ménant—(*Recherches sur la Glyptique Orientale*, p. 97, fig. 56). Two fantastic winged-beings with human heads and scorpion-like tails, face each other on either side of an object resembling an altar.   M. Ménant is no doubt right in suggesting that these weird creatures represent the Scorpion-keepers of the mysterious region beyond the seas—situated in one of the islands at the mouth of the Euphrates—who, according to the legend, guard the rising and setting of the sun.   When, in the mythical story of Gilgames, the hero, seeking Hasisadra, journeys toward the land of Mas where dwells the sage, now raised by the gods to immortality, he meets the monsters and engages in a colloquy with them.   The date of this cylinder is unknown.   We may, therefore, have here an adaptation of the Egyptian soul-bird applied by the Mesopotamian artist to the mythical guardians of the land of immortal spirits; or, which is more likely, we may have a production of pure Mesopotamian symbolism.   These *speaking* scorpions might well be represented with human heads, whilst their being endowed with wings as a proof of their supernal essence seems quite in keeping with what we know of the symbolism of the Assyrians and Babylonians.   However this may be, the creatures are primarily scorpions and not birds.

The same mythical beings are represented upon a Persian cylinder, published by Ch. Lenormant, *Mélanges d'Arch.*, III, pp. 130, etc.   There they are given lion's feet, in addition to a human head and wings—and they stand under the flying Sundisk.   V. Place, *Ninive et l'Assyrie*, 76, has also published a cylinder on which the same creatures are represented.

Among the Egyptians, the human-headed hawk,[1] in the symbolism of the historical period, belonged to the higher plane of thought which identified the soul of man with the Hawk of Horos—the Divine Spirit embodied in the sun—whose destiny it must share. Yet there is little doubt that notions more or less similar to those described above originally prevailed in Egypt. At all events, it is quite clear that, along with the belief in the soul's ultimate apotheosis, and in its diurnal journey in the solar bark, there co-existed among the people—even under the New Empire—a more homely belief[2] evidently based upon a more primitive conception of which it may be regarded as a survival, and according to which man's highest aspiration upon leaving this life, was to continue to lead in his tomb a pleasant material existence—his bird-embodied soul coming and going out at will into the day.[3]

If we remember that among people of primitive culture the spirit is identified with the breath, and the breath with the physical air—as is attested by the philology of the words used to express these ideas in many languages, ancient and modern—it becomes easy to conceive how the winged inhabitants of the aerial regions came to be looked upon as spirits by man, at a time when the stage of intellectual development he had reached made it difficult for him to deal with abstractions.

However all this may be, the human-headed bird, as an artistic

---

Indeed, according to Ménant, *loc. cit.*, I, 97, they are frequent on Chaldean and Assyrian monuments.

[1] In early times the hieroglyph for soul, Baï, was not the human-headed hawk, but a stork-like bird. See first tomb in Mariette, *Mastabas de l'Ancien Empire*, Sokar Kha biu. See also Pyramid texts in *Recueil de Travaux*, etc., Vol. III, p. 188, l. 70; p. 202, l. 209, etc. According to Gubernatis, *Zoological Mythol.*, II, 261, there is in Germany a superstition that, when storks fly around a group of persons, one of the group is about to die. And all who have traveled in Germany know the share which these birds have in the bringing of souls into the world. The same author regards owls, crows, magpies, and storks as occupying, among the Aryans, the same mythological position with regard to the dead.

[2] Comp. Maspero, *Etudes Egyptiennes*, II, p. 277.

[3] On many funeral stelæ of the XVIIIth and XIXth dynasties there occurs a formula in which the dead expresses a wish that: "I may take a walk by the edge of my basin, each day, without ceasing; that my soul may perch upon the branches of the funeral garden that I have made for myself, that I may refresh myself beneath my sycamores." Maspero, *Recueil de Travaux Relatifs à la Philologie Eg. et Ass.*, II, p. 105. 1880.

Comp. Stela C. 55 Louvre under King Aï—XVIIIth d. quoted in Maspero *Etudes Egyptiennes*, I, p. 175.

device, passed from Egypt to the Mediterranean peoples, who made use of it to illustrate many myths and legends, particularly those connected with the harpies.

These mythical beings—" daughters of the sea '"—in their origin personified, as did the Maruts of the Vedas, the storm-winds, and were evidently not the God-sent scourges which they later became, when the primeval animism of the Greeks developed into an ethical religion. It is likely that, as is the case in most primitive storm-myths, they were originally conceived as birds of prey.[2]

At first sea-born storm-winds, then messengers of Zeus, they extended comfort and protection to his favorites,[3] and executed his vengeance upon those whom he had doomed.[4] In this latter *rôle* they harassed their victims, or carried them off alive to the world's end, toward some mysterious place on the shores of the Northern Ocean.[5] It seems to be only later still that they are represented bearing away the souls of the dead; and it is probable that in the Harpy " Psychopompe," such as we see it depicted on the famous Lykian monument, known as the tomb of the Harpies,[6] we have an instance of the process so well explained by Mr. Clermont-Ganneau in his *Mythologie Iconologique,* and an evidence of the influence exercised upon the Aryan idea by the

[1] Hesiod " *Theognis*," 132 : The earth bare Pontos, 237 : Pontos and the earth bare Thaumas (*i. e.*, Wonder), 265–7 : Thaumas and Electra (*i. e.*, Lustre), daughter of Oceanus, produce Iris (*i. e.*, the Rainbow), and " the fair-tressed Harpies (the Storms), Aëllo and Ocypete, who, I ween, accompany the wind-blasts of birds with swift wings, for they are wont to fly high above the earth." In *Virgil*, Æne. iii, 245, the Harpies are numerous, and only Celaeno is mentioned by name.

[2] The Maruts are spoken of in the Vedas as warriors, as bulls, as horses, and also as birds. See, for instance, *Rig-Veda*, i, 87, 2. Hygin, Fab., xiv, says : " The three birds Harpies, Alope, Acholoe, and Ocypete, are daughters of Thaumas and Ozomene." See J. H. Cerquand, *Revue Archéol.*, 1860–1861.

[3] *Iliad*, xix, 415, 430. Zeus, wishing to soothe and comfort Achilles, calls Pallas : " As thus he spake, he sent the goddess forth, eager to do her errand. Plunging down in form a shrill-voiced Harpy, with broad wings, she cleft the air "—and feeds and strengthens the hero.

[4] See Sophocles, *Phin.* Compare Apollonius, *Argonaut*, ii, 180, etc. : "Across the clouds, suddenly appearing, the Harpies, with their claws, stole incessantly from the mouth and hands of Phineus. Often nothing remained, sometimes a little was left, that he might live in sorrow. Moreover, they cast upon those remains so detestable an odor that no one could have touched them with his lips."

[5] Comp. *Odyssey*, xx, 62–65, etc. ; Euripides, Hipp., 732 ; Strabo, vii, 302.

[6] Bas-relief of Xanthos, Brit. Mus. See Collignon, *Mytho. figurée de la Grèce*, p. 287. A terra-cotta bird, found at Dali, and now also in the Louvre, is represented in the act of bearing away a human figure in its talons. Perrot and Chipiez, *Hre. de l'Art dans l'Antiq.*, II, 591.

Egyptian form borrowed to represent it. In other words, it is the result of the grafting of the soul-bird symbol upon the Aryan myth.

Fig. 24. Siren from Cyprus. Messrs. Perrot and Chipiez, *Hist. de l'Art*, II, p. 591.

A singular form of this imaginary creature, showing the adaptation of the artistic device, with a perversion of the idea which it originally was intended to embody, was found in the island of Cyprus. and is now in the Louvre (fig. 24). It is a human-headed bird. carved in limestone, and depicted with hands, holding up pan-pipes to its

Fig. 25. Handle of bronze. Van Armenia, *Hist. de l'Art, etc.*, II, 734.

mouth. It is therefore, as already pointed out by Messrs. Perrot and Chipiez,[1] a hybrid standing between the Harpy and the Siren. and may

---

[1] *Ibid.* For forms of Greek Harpies varying from the simple, human-headed bird to the human form with bird's legs and wings, see plate in the already-quoted article by Cerquand, *Rev. Arch.*, 1860, p. 367 : see also Collignon, *loc. cit.*, 286, etc. For the introduction of the soul-bird and other Egyptian funeral practices among the Greeks, comp. Léon Heuzey, *Comptes Rendus de l'Acad. des Insc.*, 1882, p. 388, etc.

6

be regarded as illustrating one of the phases or aspects of these varying conceptions.

Among the antiquities of Van, in Armenia, are some bronze plaques in which the swinging handles of vessels were fastened. Some of these are in the shape of human-headed birds, and the one which is here given[1] may be said to have an Egyptianized expression. In this case we have reached the stage where the mythical meaning of the object represented has been entirely lost.—*i. e.*, only the decorative " motif" remains.

It is now recognized that the Mediterranean peoples at the dawn of their civilization copied many artistic forms brought to them by commerce with the outside world—often without understanding the religious ideas that had led to their creation as symbols ; that is to say, as the artistic expression of that, which to people of another race, was a deep-felt truth. Such singular composite, forms would readily strike the imagination of the Greek artist and of the Greek poet, who, in his effort to understand their meaning, often built around them innumerable legends and myths, a process in the course of which the original idea often became obscured, if not altogether lost.[2]

This is not confined to minor symbolical forms ; it extends to the Pantheon and to the mythology ; and the much quoted Har-pe-Chruti, whose childhood, represented in the conventional Egyptian way by the familiar gesture of carrying the fore-finger to the mouth, was misunderstood by the Greeks and was turned by them into Harpocrates, the God of silence ; or the myth of Bellerophon and the Chimera,[3] if perhaps the most striking and the best known, are by no means the only instances of a divine personage having more or less lost his identity before his introduction into the Greek Pantheon. There are other mythological forms which might be traced, as loans, to Egypt ; although one should tread cautiously upon such doubtful ground.

---

[1] Collections of St. Petersburg, Œuvres de Longpérier. Another is in the Coll. de Vogüé, 1, 276—*Hre. de l'Art, etc.* Perrot et Chipiez, II, p. 734. There are others in Paris and in London and similar ones have been recovered in Palestine and at Olympia, Greece. See *Arch. Zeitung*, 1879, p. 181. Mr. Holleaux, during his excavations in Greece, 1885, discovered a large brazen basin, the handle plaques of which were formed with two human headed birds, to whom the artist had also given human arms. See *Bull. de Correspondance Hellénique*, 1888, quoted in *Bull. Arch. de la Relig. grecque, Rev. des Relig.*, XX, 1, 89, 290.

[2] Comp. Clermont-Ganneau, *L'Imagerie Phénicienne et la Mythologie Iconologique*, 1880.

[3] See P. Decharme, *Mythologie de la Grèce Antique*, 1886, fig. 161. Comp. with Clermont-Ganneau, *Horus et St. George: Revue Arch.*, 1873, fig. 13.

THE SACRED TREE.

Another very interesting fragment in the collection of the University of Pennsylvania, also from Tel-Defenneh (*i. e.*, seventh century B. C. fig. 26), is the broken neck of an amphora-shaped vase of red incised

Fig. 26. Potsherd from Daphnæ, in the Museum of the University of Pennsylvania.

pottery, decorated with a most significant design, of which many adaptations or corruptions are, like the ancient soul-bird just referred to, in common use to-day. The variations which this one artistic theme furnished the Mediterranean peoples are well-nigh infinite; and it is, therefore, scarcely surprising to find it constantly applied by our modern artists under different names :

The hylix-pattern—as Mr. Birch calls it,[1] the honeysuckle design— as it is termed in our schools of decorative art, the anthemion—its classical name; or, according to the French name in which, strangely enough. the original intention has been preserved through all these centuries: the " Palmette."

Whatever may have been the history of the symbolism represented in this type of the sacred tree—which is evidently a composite one— our potsherd teaches us that, in this highly conventional form, it exercised a powerful influence upon the decorative art of the Mediterranean peoples, and supplied them with an endless variety of designs.

From at least the ninth century B. C. it was a familiar object on the walls of the palaces of Nineveh[2] (fig. 27). In early times the sacred

---

[1] *Ancient Pottery*, pp. 303-5.
[2] Layard's *Monum.*, first series, pl. 7. Only the top of the tree is here given.

Fig. 27. Top of sacred tree. From Layard's *Monuments of Nineveh*, 1st series, pl. vii

palm-tree seems to have been generally drawn in its natural shape—
or, at all events, in a more simple emblematic form.[1] It is obvious that
foreign artisans could not have been inspired by the wall-decorations of
the temples, palaces, or tombs of distant lands, and that such designs
as served them as models must have reached them by means of portable
manufactures. There is little doubt that the inordinate use which the
Assyrians made of the "palmette" in the ninth, eighth, and seventh
centuries B. C.—*i. e.*, during the period of their most stirring warlike and commercial activity in a westerly direction—accounts for
its great popularity in Asia Minor, and among the inhabitants of
the basin of the Mediterranean Sea at about this time.

If we make due allowance for the difference in the execution of the
two pieces above given—one a carefully-sculptured bas-relief, in
carving which the Assyrian artist was treating the conventional
symbol of his own religion, the other a rough sketch, drawn upon the
neck of an ordinary pottery vessel by a foreign artisan, copying what,
to him, seemed simply a decorative device—we shall see that the latter

[1] See Ménant. *Recherch. sur la Glyptiq. Orientale*, p. 140. fig. 86. Cylinder of
Dungi, son of Urkham; and another, p. 142. fig. 87; another, p. 189. fig. 120, although a well-drawn palm tree, is set up on a sort of altar, and approaches an
emblematic form. Many examples might be given of very ancient forms, more or less
conventionalized.

has made what may be considered a very fair attempt at adapting the well-known symbol to his artistic purposes.

This comes out much more distinctly in the black and white copy

Fig. 28. Potsherd from Daphnæ. From Mr. Flinders-Petrie, *Tanis*, 11, pl. xxxi, fig. 4.

of the design, taken from Mr. Petrie's work (fig. 28) than it does in the photograph, where the red coloring of part of the pattern causes the outline to be indistinct.

The same design occurs, much more neatly executed, upon a Greek amphora signed by Nicosthenes, published by Mr. Klein,[1] and the approximate date of which is circa 500, B. C.

It is worthy of note that a sherd also signed by this artist was recovered at Naukratis.[2] This fact, viewed in connection with the absence[3] at Daphnæ and Naukratis, of the types of decorated pottery which elsewhere preceded the introduction of the "Oriental" style,[4] gives us a hint as to the possible influence of the Delta school of art upon the work of Nicosthenes. Indeed, doubt has been expressed as to his having been an Athenian.[5]

Mr. E. B. Tylor, in an interesting article, recently published,[6] has gone far toward proving that the large winged-figures which have become so familiar to us from their frequent occurrence on the bas-reliefs of the Babylonian and Assyrian palaces, where they are depicted standing in front of the sacred tree, touching it with a cone-like object which they hold in their hand—represent the divine act of fertilizing the tree over which they are supposed to shake the pollen of the full-blown male blossom (fig. 29). To the people of Mesopotamia

[1] *Vasen mit Meistersign.*, p. 30.

[2] *Naukratis*, Part I, p. 53.

[3] *Naukratis*, Part I, p. 49. Chapter on Pottery by Mr. Cecil Smith.

[4] Although certain survivals of the "Geometric" type of decoration had remained to show that the time was not very far off when it was in vogue. Comp. Chapter on the *Pottery from the Temenos of Aphrodite*, by Mr. E. A. Gardner. *Naukratis*, Part II. p. 56.

[5] Comp. Cecil Smith in *Naukratis*, Part I, p. 52. See an excellent article by Mr. H. A. Tubbs in Smith's *Dict. of Greek and Roman Antiq.*, p. 929.

[6] *Proceedings of the Soc. of Biblical Arch.*, 1890.

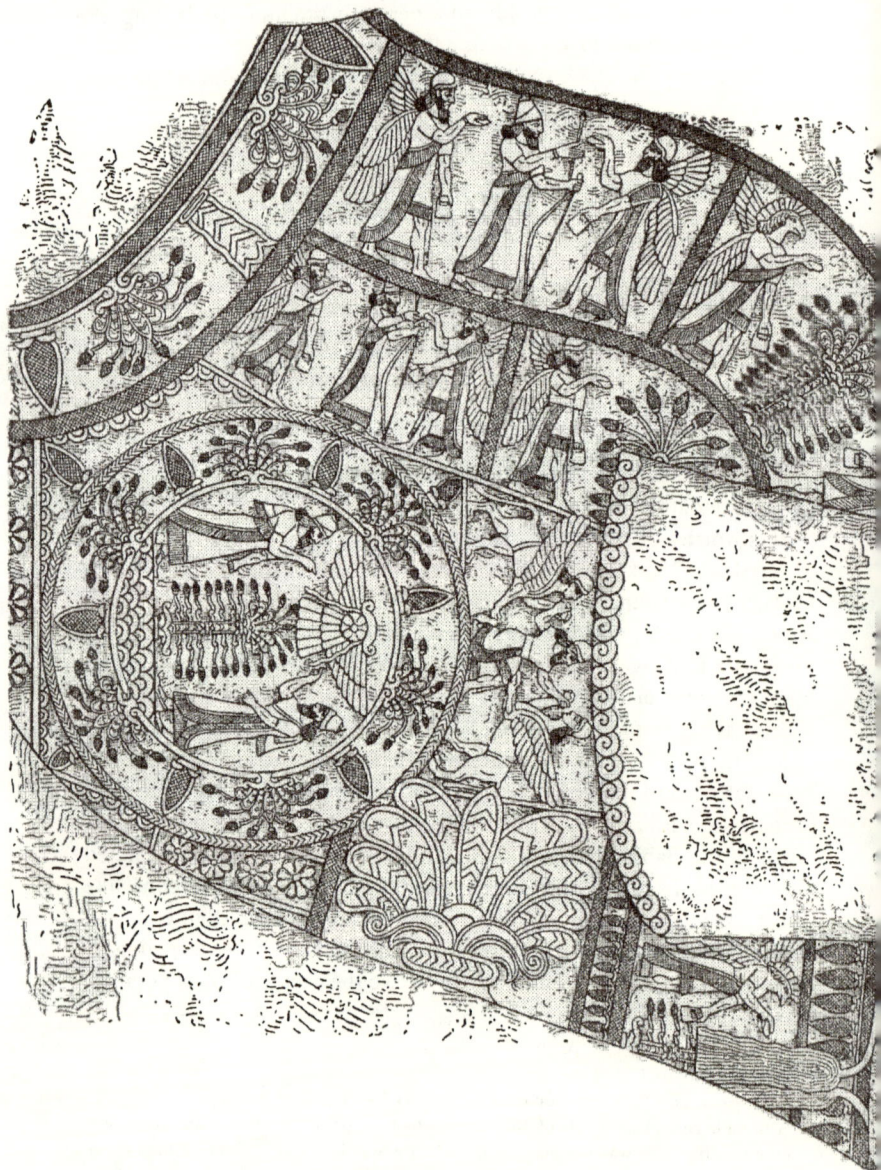

Fig. 29. Robe. From Layard's *Monuments of Nineveh.*

the fruit of the palm was the " staff of life." The wine made from it
" made glad the heart of man ;"[1] and the failure of the annual crop

---

[1] Sayce, *Hibbert Lectures*, 1887, p. 242.

meant famine in the land. Therefore, according to Mr. Tylor, the gods, by the fulfilment of this act were thought to insure the life and prosperity of their worshippers.

This view receives strong confirmation from the observation of the palm trees, figured on the monuments as natural objects in the landscape. These present so close a resemblance to the *palmette* that the latter can scarcely be called a conventionalized form. See Layard's *Monuments*, etc., plates 58, 72, 41, 43, 49, etc. This is particularly the case when, as on a cylinder published by J. Ménant, (*loc. cit.*, p. 191, fig. 121,) the palm tree, although represented as a natural object, is drawn with a short trunk. In the Assyrian landscapes the palm trees have as many as 11 or 13 palms, yet some are represented with as few as 6—and the usual number is 7 or 9—*i. e.*, numbers commonly exhibited by the conventional design.

Although there is every likelihood that Mr. Tylor has come very close to solving the problem, it seems likely that we have in the conventional representation of the tree, so common during the last centuries of the great Assyrian Empire, a syncretism of the various sacred trees worshipped throughout the land.[1]

That there were several of these seems certain, and a close inspection of the artistic renderings of the tree of life on the ancient cylinders reveals the fact that, although the palm is by far the most frequently dealt with, others are depicted which apparently should not be confused with it. For instance, a cylinder found at Tello by Mr. de Sarzec,[2] seems to represent a simple Ashêrah, topped by branches that somewhat resemble stag's horns, and decorated with long streamers.

Others represent trees, at the end of each naked branch of which is a cone.[3] Perhaps we have in these the cedar, the sacred tree of

[1] Mr. Sayce suggests (*loc. cit.*, 242,) that the palm and the cedar—the sacred tree of Eridu—may have become merged into one by the later Babylonians, or that the palm tree may have succeeded the older cedar tree. This latter hypothesis (p. 240) does not seem to me a likely one, as the palm appears on very ancient cylinders. The first seems far more probable. Mr. Sayce also recalls the fact that among the Western Semites there was a tradition that mentioned two trees: the tree of knowledge and the tree of life. See Genesis iii, 21-24. "And the Lord said: behold the man is become like one of us, to know good and evil: and now lest he put forth his hand and take also of the tree of life, and eat and live forever." . . . "So He drove out the man; and He placed at the east of the garden of Eden—cherubims and a flaming sword, which turned every way to keep the way of the tree of life."

[2] Léon Heuzey, *La masse d'Armes*, Paris, 1887, quoted by Mr. Goblet d'Alviella, *La Migration des Symboles*, Paris, 1891. p. 171.

[3] J. Ménant, *Recherches sur la Glyptique Orient.*, p. 65, fig. 5, gives a cylinder on

Eridu, which at all times played a conspicuous part in the magic of the Babylonians.[1] Mr. Sayce[2] also quotes a passage in which the " divine lady of Edin " is mentioned as the " Goddess of the tree of life " in the Akkadian of N. Babylonia, and as the " Goddess of the vine " in the Sumerian of S. Babylonia. So that, if this is correct, the sacred tree would appear to have also been identified with the vine.

Moreover, according to Sir George Birdwood,[3] certain forms of the climbing plant wound around the sacred tree on Assyrian bas-reliefs closely approach the " Asclepias acida "—i. e., the sacred plant or tree of life, from which Hindus and Iranians both derived their immortal Soma or Haoma.

On the other hand, the cone is sometimes held up—not only over a tree—but to the face of human figures or objects which are not palm-trees—or the conventional gesture is made before the tree without the cone being held in the hand of the figure[4] (fig. 29 furnishes examples of this). And Mr. Goblet d'Alviella has very justly observed[5] that the cone is used in very much the same manner as is the Ankh—or " life "-sign by the Egyptian gods—and obviously with a life-imparting intention.

The evidence seems therefore to point to the fact that our symbol, in its later conventional shape, was a complex one. That originally it was closely associated with the great nature-goddess, and that the scenes in which it so conspicuously appears were symbolical of the universal generative and reproductive powers of deified nature, seems to

which palms are represented, and on the same cylinder a seated god holds in his hand a stem with branches, at the end of each of which is a cone. Such trees are represented as natural objects in the landscape in historical bas-reliefs (See Layard's *Monuments*, p. 33, p. 39, fig. 1–46, fig. 1), showing that they were intentionally thus depicted.

[1] Mr. F. Lenormant (*Les Origines de l'Hist.*, I, p. 84, gives the following text from *Cuneif. Insc.* W. A., IV, pl. 162): " Take a vase, put in it some water, put in it some white cedar wood, place in it the charm that comes from Eridu, and thus complete the virtue of the enchanted waters." Another text given by the same author says : " Take the fruit of the cedar, and present it to the face of the patient ; the cedar is the tree that gives the pure magic and repels the unfriendly demons—ever ready to ensnare "—*loc. cit.*, 83–84. Comp. Sayce, *Hibbert Lectures*, 1887, p. 242. It was upon the heart at the core of the cedar tree that the name of Ea was inscribed, and it was associated with the magical arts and the secrets of heaven. Only the initiated could taste its fruit.

[2] *Loc. cit.*, p. 260. Note.

[3] *Industrial Arts of India*, Part II, p. 430.

[4] (*Antiq. R. M.* I Part III, pp. 362, 363, 364, 369, etc.)

[5] *La Migration des Symboles*, p. 180. Comp. above, p. 86, pl. 29.

be implied in the words of an ancient hymn of Eridu, in which it is described : [1] " In Eridu (a stalk) grew overshadowing; in a holy place did it become green ;

" Its root was of white crystal which stretched toward the deep ; (before) Ea was its course in Eridu, teeming with fertility ;

" Its seat was the [central] place of the earth; its foliage (?) was the couch of Zikum [the primeval] mother,

" Into the heart of its holy house which spread its shade like a forest hath no man entered.

" (There is the home) of the mighty mother who passes across the sky.

" [In] the midst of it was Tammuz." [2]

Mr. d'Alviella suggests that this hymn may throw light upon the meaning of the group so often formed by the tree and the winged figures under the sun-disk, from which worshippers seem to draw down the life-giving rays of the sun upon the symbol, the whole scene being emblematic of the universal divine fecundity.   It may be worthy of note in connection with this, that Dr. Richter has found a votive-offering of a sacred-tree in the temenos of Aphrodite at Chytroi, Cyprus.   (See *Ancient Places of Worship in Kypros*, p. 48, pl. xvii.)

That even as a common-place decorative design, the sacred palm retained its meaning for the Assyrian artist, is hinted at in the ornamental detail of the gorgeous robe worn by Assur-nazir-pal on a bas-relief of the palace (fig. 30) of Nimrud.[3]   On this, the workman has detached the palm in its most conventional shape, to form the centre of a group in which two goats or two winged bulls are alternately represented bending the knee before the sacred object.   We, therefore, have here the transitional stage of the emblem—adapted and used for ordinary purposes, just as the cross often is with us—and which, in its purely decorative character, was carried by commerce over the entire region to which it had direct or indirect access.

The rosette, which, in Mesopotamian art, was conventionally used as a symbol of the sun, had probably a similar history ; and its emblematic meaning in Mesopotamia, as well as the common use which its inhabitants made of it for purposes of decoration, justify its being considered a typical Mesopotamian symbol.

---

[1] *Hibbert Lectures*, 1, '87, Sayce, p. 238. Comp. F. Lenormant *Orig. de l' Hist.*, II, p. 104.

[2] The Sun-God regarded as either the son or the husband of the Nature-Goddess.

[3] Layard. *Monuments*, etc., I series, p. 43.

Whatever may have been the genesis of similar designs in other regions [1]—whether they may be traced to floral or to geometrical forms —there is no room for doubting that its origin, on the banks of the·

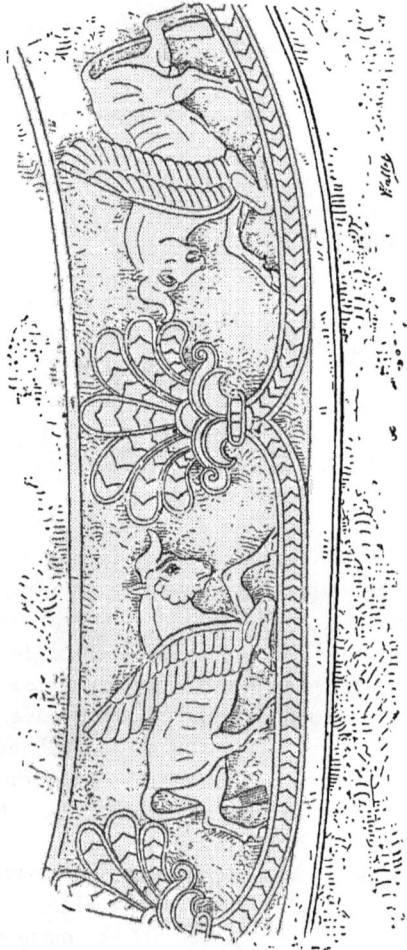

Fig. 30. Design from Robe.   Layard's *Monuments of Nineveh*, I series. p. 43.

Euphrates, must be traced to the eight-rayed star which, from the very earliest times to which we have access in Chaldea, was the ideogram

---

[1] Mr. Murray, *Handbook of Arch.*, p. 77, has very properly pointed out that the rosette designs could be readily arrived at independently, without any conscious borrowing on the part of the artist.

for "god." Even as early as the time when the Tello monuments were erected, the star-symbol occurs in the conventional form of a star-rosette enclosed in a disk.[1] Later, a common form of representation for the sun is a four-ray star between the rays of which flame-like streaks are depicted.[2] And although the variety of form presented by the symbol in the course of time is almost endless, and it tends to lose its identity in the floral form; the numerous star-types survived to indicate its evolution from the hieroglyph for "god."[3]

We have at the Museum of the University of Pennsylvania a lime-stone bas-relief of the time of Khu-en-aten,[4] when Mesopotamian influence was, as shown by the discoveries at Tel-el-Amarna, very strong in Egypt, which represents a priest worshipping the sun-disk: This is simply depicted in the form of a floral rosette from which rays depend. Although it occurs early in Egypt, the rosette was never used there to represent the sun, and it only becomes common as a decorative design from the beginning of the New Empire. Then, however, it is vulgarized and frequently met with. For instance, there are, also in the collection of the University, some tiles from a palace of Rameses III at Tel-el-Yahudiyeh,[5] the design of which is identical with that to be seen on some tiles from Nineveh, now in the Louvre, and on which the wheel pattern likewise alternates with the floral rosette.

Mr. Goodyear[7] has offered a very probable suggestion as to the origin of the Egyptian rosette: He proposes to see in the dried-up ovary stigma of the lotus after seeding, the model from which the Egyptian artists derived their floral design. There is no doubt that the natural object. as given by Mr. Goodyear, bears a striking resemblance to the type which I have distinguished by the term of "floral," which makes its

---

[1] Mr. de Sarzec, *Découvertes en Chaldée*, pl. 46, No. 7.

[2] Stèle of Nabu habal idin. Brit. Mus. disc. by Mr. Rassam. See Ménant, *loc. cit.*, 246. Here the simple eight-rayed star is the special symbol of Ishtar.

[3] See, for instance, Layard *Monum.*, pl. 42, where the star and floral varieties are each represented on the bracelets of two great winged figures of the palace of Nimrud. Plate 13 furnishes us with every possible variety: from the true solar eight-rayed star type to the later floral designs.

[4] Sent by Mr. W. M. Flinders-Petrie and found by him at Gurob.

[5] Sent by the "Egypt. Exp. Fund" in 1890.

[6] See Perrot and Chipiez, *Hre, de l'Art*, etc., II, p.

[7] *Am. Jour. of Arch.*, 1888, p. 290, fig. 14. "The Egyptian origin of the Ionic Capital and the Greek Anthemion."

Since the above was written, Mr. Goodyear in his work, the *Grammar of the Lotus*, 1892, has stated that Mr. Newberry also coincides in this opinion.

appearance on the banks of the Euphrates toward the close of the second millennium B. C.

In connection with this suggestion, it is interesting to find that the Rosette-Sun-disk on the monument of Khu-en-aten, to which I have alluded above, is precisely of the pronounced "stigma" type. It would thus seem as though, at the time when Mesopotamian influence was strong enough to overcome the hieratic traditions of the native Egyptian artists, to such an extent as to lead them to represent the sun-disk after the fashion of the Asiatics, the Egyptian Rosette. brought into prominence by the novel use to which it had been adapted, had reacted upon the form used in Mesopotamia where it found its way and became popular.

This was the time (fifteenth century B. C.) when, as is shown by the recent discoveries at Tel-el-Amarna, Egypt was most subject to foreign influences;[1] and when the Babylonian scribes attached to the Court conducted a wide correspondence in the neo-Babylonian character with allied and tributary rulers of distant Semitic states. It is therefore likely that it is also at this time that many Egyptian artistic forms were grafted upon the symbolism of Asia; a process which gave rise to the mixed style of decoration so characteristic of the art of the Assyrian empire; and which. in the days of its supremacy and with the development of Phœnician commerce. spread over the Western world. At all events, the cuneiform tablets found at Tel-el-Amarna reveal a constant and direct interchange of industrial and natural products between Egypt and Mesopotamia; trees. brazen vases, bulls, etc., were, at this time, sent by the Asiatic kings in exchange for gold. stone-tables, Egyptian wares, and even skilled servants.[2]

A careful comparison of the remains of the Valley of the Euphrates with those of the Valley of the Nile cannot fail to bring with it the conviction that the two civilizations which they represent developed independently. If we make the proper allowance for such facts as are sufficiently explained by certain aspirations common to the human race. for the expression of which primitive arts and industries offer necessarily restricted means ; and by a general likeness in the external circumstances of life that engenders common needs, born of common physical conditions. we shall find differences more fundamental in the

---

[1] See Mr. Petrie's letter in the London *Academy*, April 9th, 1892.

[2] *Proc. of the Soc. Biblical Arch.*, 1888-9, June 5th, p. 588, etc. Mr. Budge gives the contents of letters from Burra-buryas, King of Babylon, and from Alashya, king of Mitanni, etc., in which such transactions are mentioned.

manner in which the men of each region worked out the problems set before them, than the analogies that are apt, at first sight, to strike a superficial observer.

Contact, of course, there was—and a mutual exchange of thought and of industrial commodities took place, probably at a much earlier period even than that which we have been considering. But the loans that resulted from such intercourse[1] are beginning to be easier to detect ; and with the progress of science, as we are permitted to penetrate more deeply into the inner thoughts that inspired these men, and which they embodied in their art, we may more readily distinguish that which belongs to the spirit of each race, from that which contact with others grafted upon the original stock of primeval ideas.

But to return to our potsherd. This fragment from Tel-Defenneh, dating from the seventh century B. C.—*i. e.*, towards the close of a period of immense Babylonian and Assyrian activity—enables us to trace the filiation of a long series of ancient and modern designs, to the sacred tree. It very nearly approaches the well-known conventional form of the Assyrian symbol, yet contains all the elements which, in time, were transformed for the common purposes of decoration :[2] and

Fig. 31. *Naukratis*, Part II, pl. vii, fig. 4.

we are reminded that we are on Egyptian soil by the lotus-like form assumed by the portion of the design which, in the Assyrian symbol,

[1] Mr. Léon Heuzey. *Les Origines Orientales de l'Art*, Vol. I, pp. 6 and 25, admits a distant Egyptian influence upon the art of Tello, but regards it as independently developed, and believes that in many particulars it betrays a spirit opposed to Egyptian methods.

[2] Comp. with the remarkable Cypriote form of the sacred tree, highly conventionalized and much altered, published by Dr. Max Ohnefalsch Richter (*Journal of Hellenic Studies*, Vol. V, p. 105)

is a horn-like scroll.   This lotus-form soon defines itself on other
designs, and eventually becomes the favorite type of decoration used by

Fig. 32. *Naukratis*, Part I, pl. vii, fig. 15.

the artist-potters of Daphnæ and Naukratis [1]—the same elements being
used to produce different effects (figs. 31 and 32).

Fig. 33. *Defenneh*, xxxi, fig. 1.

On the neck of a similar amphora, reproduced by Mr. Flinders-
Petrie [2] (fig. 33), the scroll supporting the palm, instead of stretching
upward, as in our sherd, is tightly coiled beneath it.   The greater or less
loosening of these coils will in turn furnish the Greek artist with the
many graceful running varieties of the pattern which are still in use
to-day in our art-schools, and which have not been improved upon.

In comparing the decorative motives used by the artists of Thera,
Melos, Rhodes, Cyprus, etc., and the Delta, it is very interesting to
note how the same artistic elements, brought to them by outside influences, were appropriated and turned to account by each local school
of art, which impressed upon them its own original stamp.

[1] *Naukratis*, E. A. Gardner, Part II; *Ibid.*, pl. vii, fig. 4; pl. xi, fig. 2; plate viii, fig.
5. Also, *Defenneh*, see *Tanis*, Vol. II, pls. 7 and 27, fig. 3, and pl. 18, fig. 4.
[2] *Tanis*, Part II (*Defenneh*), pl. xxxi, fig. 1. Compare with the vases found in the
island of Melos (Conze *Melische Thongefässe*), and with those found at Thera and
Kamiros.

The fact that several of the ceramic forms found at Tel-Defenneh by Mr. Petrie are considered by him as intermediate between the well-known Egyptian shapes and the true Greek types found elsewhere, and that these intermediate forms are often decorated with the most archaic designs, derives its principal interest from the history and the geographical position of the site on which they were found.

Fig. 34. Daphnæ. *Tanis*, Part II, pl. xvii, fig. 3.

Tel-Defenneh,[1] the Daphnæ of the Greeks, was situated on the edge of the desert and was a stronghold protecting the road to Syria. According to Herodotus[2] it is at Daphnæ that Sesostris—*i. e.*, Rameses II—was received and feted upon his return from his victorious Syrian campaign, and narrowly escaped death at the hands of his brother, Armaïs. But although Mr. Petrie, while excavating the

[1] *Tanis*, Part II (Defenneh), W. M. Flinders-Petrie.
[2] II, 107.

mound of Daphnæ, came upon the remains of a baked-brick foundation wall of much earlier date than the other ruins, which he judged, from a certain analogy with a similar structure met with at Tel-Nebesheh, must date from the epoch of the Ramessids, the objects recovered there, and the ruins among which they were found, only go back to the reign of Psammetichus I.

It is outside the gates of Daphnæ that this monarch established the

Fig. 35. Daphnæ. *Tanis*, Part II, pl. xviii, fig. 4.

camp of his mercenaries, the Ionians and Karians, with whose help he had overcome the forces of the Dodecarchy, and had inaugurated the XXVI Dynasty, who ruled Egypt from Saïs in the Delta.[1] To judge from the character of the ruins explored by Mr. Petrie, the town of Daphnæ became far more Greek than Egyptian. Moreover its geographical position as an outpost on the eastern frontier of

[1] Herod. II, 154.

Egypt brought its inhabitants into close relations with their Asiatic neighbors, and it is probable that many immigrants from Syria sought refuge in the Greco-Egyptian city at the time of Nebuchadnezzar's invasion of Judæa.[1]

After the defeat of Apries, (570-565 B. C.) Amasis removed the Greek troops to Memphis and replaced them at Daphnæ by an Egyptian garrison. At the same time he restricted all foreign commerce to Naukratis, in the Western Delta ; and, from this time forth, Naukratis retained the monopoly of foreign trade, which its close proximity to Saïs, the seat of Egyptian government at that time, favored. Daphnæ, stripped of all that had contributed to its prosperity, then entered upon its decline ; and all the pottery of Greek or mixed forms recovered among its ruins can therefore be chronologically restricted to a limited period—*i. e.*, 670-570 B. C.—according to Mr. Petrie,[2] no Greek pottery found there can be assigned a date later than 550 B. C. In the time of Herodotus[3] a Persian garrison held Daphnæ.

We are here, therefore, in possession of all the necessary facts bearing upon the history of our potsherds; and it is most instructive to find the ancient pottery of Greek or mixed types, made by Greek potters of the seventh and sixth centuries before our era, upon Egyptian soil, decorated with designs inspired not only by Egyptian, but by various Asiatic influences : The lotus-bud, worked into numerous different conceits, the Sphynx, which has already lost its Egyptian repose and gravity and gained in grace all that the artistic Greek has caused him to lose in dignity and in depth of meaning: and the Soul-bird, found side by side not only with the sacred tree of Mesopotamia, but even with certain decorations of Amazons declared by the highest authority upon the subject, Mr. Murray,[4] to be of Persian origin.

The active traffic of the period, which produced the eclecticism in art so noticeable among the Greek colonists of Daphnæ, is further illustrated by the result of Mr. Petrie's excavations at Tel-Nebireh, the site of ancient Naukratis, the Greco-Egyptian emporium of the sixth century B. C.

Here the explorers found traces of iron foundries and of a factory of pottery, etc., which show the town to have been a great centre not only of trade, as was already known, but also of manufacture.

[1] W. M. Flinders-Petrie, *Tanis*, II, p. 49.

[2] W. M. Flinders-Petrie, *Tanis*, II, p. 52.

[3] II, 30.

[4] See *Chapter on Pottery*, by A. S. Murray, in the Vol. of *Tanis*, II, Nebesheh and Defenneh, p. 70.

98

From the factory of pottery and amulets we have in the Museum of the University, not only scarabs and other amulets, but the moulds themselves in which these were cast, and lumps of the coloring matter used to give to the glaze its particular hue. Among the numerous scarabs collected upon this spot by Mr. Petrie were types previously found in the Island of Rhodes.[1] These, executed by foreign workmen had, in many cases, betrayed their non-Egyptian manufacture by certain peculiarities of treatment, or by the faulty rendering of the hieroglyphs. At other points of the basin of the Mediterranean, objects of Egyptian origin have also from time to time been found. Although there is no doubt that many specimens of Egyptian art and industry found their way to different points of the civilized world through direct or indirect intercourse, many centuries before the foundation of Naukratis,[2] it is nevertheless evident that we have here the centre of trade where a large number of those which have been recovered were manufactured, and whence they were afterward distributed ; possibly, in the course of time, serving as models for local workmen to imitate.

In the tombs of Etruria many objects have been exhumed, some of undoubted Egyptian manufacture, others not so typically Egyptian, which were thought, at the time of their discovery, to be foreign imitations of Egyptian models.[3] That which makes these particularly interesting in connection with the discoveries at Naukratis, is the presence among them of vases of green porcelain glaze—a glaze characteristic of the last millennium B. C.,[4] and which was very common in Egypt about the time of the establishment of the Greek colonies in the Delta, when Daphnæ and Naukratis became active centres. In the Polledrara tomb, near Vulci, such porcelain vases were found, inscribed with hieroglyphics of unfamiliar form, which had obviously been drawn by workmen unacquainted with the Egyptian language. Moreover, on one of the incised ostrich eggs also found there, was cut the Greek letter "A" in a form that precisely coincides with the writing of the Greek colonists settled at Naukratis in the VIIth century, B.C.[5]

---

1 *Naukratis*, Part I, p. 47.

2 At Yalisos [Rhodes] where the tombs are of the most archaic type, a scarab of Amenhotep III was found. Duncker, *Hist. of Greece*, p. 53. See also for evidences of Egyptian influence in Cyprus under the 18th D., Dr. M. Ohnefalsch-Richter in *Verhandlungen Berlin Anth. Gesells.*, Jan. 1st, 1891 ; in "*Die Nation*," June 21st, 1891, and in *Mittheil. der Anthrop. Gesells. in Wien*, Nov., Dec., 1890.

3 Birch, *Ancient Pottery*, 433, quot. *Micali Monumenti inèditi, Tavola* VII.

4 *Catalog. Brit. Mus.*, p. 74, 1888.

5 Murray. *Handbook of Greek Arch.*, p. 56. Figures of the God Bes and of Osiris

This alone must date the tomb, even though a scarab of Psammetichus I. had not been recovered among these objects.

Scarabs of glazed ware, one of which bore the cartouche of the same
king, unguent vases, and other objects of Egyptian origin were
recovered at Capo di Selvo on the site of ancient Tharras on the west
coast of Sardinia, and among these there also occur vases of the pale
green porcelain glaze already referred to.[1]

Mr. Wiedemann[2] mentions an ushabti of the Vth or VIth century
B. C. which was discovered some 20 years ago among some Roman
antiquities in Würtemberg; he also mentions other Egyptian objects,
manufactured some time between the VIIth and the IVth centuries B. C.,
which have been exhumed near Cologne and Bonn. Others have
been found in Gaul. Whatever may be the time at which the latter
objects found their way to the distant lands where they have been discovered, all these facts tend to show that the commerce with Egypt
was an extensive one—not limited to Asia Minor and the neighboring
islands, but fully established and carrying far and wide the products of
Egyptian civilization.

It is therefore impossible to doubt the influence which the art of
Naukratis must have exercised over that of neighboring peoples, or
the share which the great Græco-Egyptian mart had in bringing about
the blending of exotic forms with the decorative designs peculiar to
the Mediterranean nations.

ORIENTAL DESIGN.

That the artist-potters of Naukratis no more confined themselves to
Greece or Egypt for their models than did their fellow-workmen of
Daphnæ, is shown by the very handsome potsherds herewith given,
which continue the story told by our Daphnæ pottery.

On the Naukratis vases, as on those recovered at Kamiros, the disposition of the decoration—which is divided into concentric zones—
each zone developing its own theme, has been traced, by all who have
made a study of the subject, to Assyrian influence.

and Isis, as well as two Egyptian scarabs of green glaze, regarded by Mr. Steindorf
as dating from not earlier than the XXVIth dynasty, have recently been recovered by
Signor Falchi from ancient interments at Vetulonia on the Poggio alla Guardia. *Am.
Journ. of Arch.*, Dec., 1891, p. 511.

[1] De la Marmora, *Voy. en Sardaigne*, II, 359. See also Perrot et Chipiez *Hre. de
l'Art, etc.*, IV, and Birch, *Ancient Pottery*, p. 47, quoting p. 15, *Bull. Arch. Sard.*, 1857,
p. 139.

[2] *Eine Statuette aus Würtemberg*, 1887.

As this artistic ware was never manufactured by either the Egyptians or the Assyrians, the generally accepted opinion as to the manner in which this style of decoration reached the artists of the Greek colonies, is that it was brought to them on Assyrian textiles, through Phœnician commerce. Mr. Murray[1] regards this peculiar type of pottery as having been invented by the colonial potters, who came into more direct contact with the East, and he thinks that it later found its way to Greece. He has also pointed out that the meanders, rosettes, and other geometri-

Fig. 36. *Naukratis.* Potsherd, in the Museum of the University of Pennsylvania.

cal designs which are scattered over the background of these animal scenes, are but a survival of the "geometrical" style characteristic of the Archaic Greek pottery, which the artist-potters could not bring themselves suddenly to discard altogether, when the new designs furnished them by Oriental textiles, gave rise to the type of decoration which we are now considering.

One can but concur in these general conclusions which have been

[1] *Loc. cit.*, p. 61.

arrived at through much learning and a serious study of the question.
Yet there seems to be another and more direct way than that furnished by the Asiatic textiles, through which these Oriental designs
may have reached the Mediterranean artists, and may have suggested

Fig. 37. *Naukratis.* Potsherd, in the Museum of the University of Pennsylvania.

to them the highly specialized class of pottery known as the incised
painted "Oriental" ware, by placing under their very eyes vessels
upon which such devices were employed with telling effect.

On the accompanying potsherds, we have good specimens of the

Fig. 38. *Naukratis.* Potsherd, in the Museum of the University of Pennsylvania.

Naukratis incised type. The subjects are divided into zones. Here
a series of grazing deer, ibexes or antelopes (figs. 36 and 37), not
elongated out of all proportion—as on some of the Kamiros, Cyprus,
and other Island vases, but well drawn in their natural shape and

executed in polychrome; above or below are series of wild animals, divided by well-defined conventional lines; whilst on the smaller sherd we have the well-known Asiatic theme of a lion attacking an ibex (fig. 38). In all these, the animals, their attitudes, the mode of

Fig. 39. Bronze Patera, from the N. W. Palace of Nimrud. Layard, *Monuments of Nineveh*, I series, plate 60.

treatment, and above all the incised outline of the principal figures—apparently a superfluous feature of the well-drawn painted design—immediately recall not only the embroideries on the Assyrian textiles, but more particularly the decoration to be seen on some of the engraved metal bowls called "paterae," which have been discovered in such numbers in and out of Mesopotamia.[1]

Those to which I am particularly referring were found by Mr. Layard in the northwest palace of Nimrud, founded by Assur-nazir-pal (ab. 880 B. C.), but afterward repaired and inhabited by Sargon II (circa 740 B. C.). So that the objects found there should probably not be referred to a date earlier than the latter reign.

Some of these bowls are engraved with Egyptian subjects, and reproduce Hathor-heads, Sphinxes, scarabs, feathers of truth, cartouches, and even hieroglyphs.[2] But, even in the most Egyptian among them, there is something unfamiliar in the curve of the wings or in the disposition of the hieroglyphs, etc., that betrays their foreign origin, and convinces the most superficial observer of their non-Egyptian "provenance." Some present mixed forms; but others, such as the one here given,[3] (fig. 39) are decorated with processions of animals, in what has been termed by students of ancient art "true Mesopotamian style." And the bulls, the ibex, the leopard, the griffin, etc., which are represented either grazing or fighting—their attitudes, their general expression, are so similar to those on our potsherds, that it is difficult to avoid the inference that the men who designed each were inspired by the same models; and that the engraved outlines on the metal bowls suggested to the potter-artists the incised lines which they applied to their pottery.

It had long ago been suggested by competent authorities,[4] that the original models of these bronze "paterae" first came from Mesopotamia, and were exported into Syria, where the industry became naturalized and perfected; use being made—for the sake of obtaining variety—not only of the usual Assyrian theme, but of those Egyptian and mixed designs that at one time proved so perplexing to antiquaries. Now, we know that, through the enterprise of the Phœnicians, and through their commercial relations with the trade

---

[1] For the influence of metal vessels upon Island and Greek pottery, compare Mr. Cecil Smith in *Journ. Hell. Studies*, V, 233, and in *Arch. Zeitung*, 1881.

[2] Layard, *Monuments*, II series, plates 59 to 68.

[3] *Ibid.*, pl. 60, Perrot and Chipiez, *Hre. de l'Art*, etc., II, 741.

[4] Perrot and Chipiez, *Hre. de l'Art*, etc., II, p. 749.

centres of the Mediterranean Coast, these exotic forms were scattered
abroad, and not only became known far and wide, but furnished local
artists with models for the ornamentation of their own wares. Even
as far as Etruria this type of decoration is found. On an Etruscan
figure of hammered bronze, found near Vulci (Polledrara tomb), and
now in the British Museum,[1] the skirt of the statuette is ornamented
with a zone of animals in relief. We have already seen[2] that the
objects recovered in this locality were associated with Egyptian antiquities dating from the VIIth century B. C., and Mr. Murray[3] regards
this figure as representing Etruscan art prior to 600 B. C.

The conspicuous place which the stag and other cervidæ occupy on
the vases decorated with these designs would, alone, point to Mesopotamia, where, if we may judge from its early and constant representation on the cylinders, this class of animal played, from the earliest
times, an important part in the religious symbolism of the people.

According to Mr. Sayce,[4] the antelope was particularly connected
with Ea, the great god of Eridu, to whom the gazelle likewise seems
to have borne some relation.[5]

The latter animal was also identified with the God of Nipur, Mullil,
who was called the "gazelle god,"[6] and with whom the goat was
associated.[7] Indeed, it is apparent that the primitive zoölogists of
Mesopotamia did not discriminate very closely between ibex and oryx
goats and the cervidæ.[8]

Deer and antelopes of various kinds were held sacred in different
parts of the Semitic world. They were not forbidden food, but bore
a relation to certain divinities. Troops of sacred gazelles occur down
to a late day at the sanctuaries of Mecca and Tabala, and in the island
spoken of by Arrian.[9] Stags and gazelles occur as sacred symbols in

---

[1] See *Hist. of Greek Sculpture*, I, p. 85, 2d ed.

[2] See above, p. 98.

[3] *Handbook of Greek Archæology*, p. 241, fig. 82.

[4] *Lectures on the Origin and Growth of Religion, as Illustrated by the Religion of the Ancient Babylonians*, 1887, p. 280, quoting W. A. I., II, 55, 27–30, and *Ibid*, II, 62, 39.

[5] A. H. Sayce, *loc. cit.*, p. 283, quoting W. A. I., II, 6, 7; 59, 5; 55, 31–33.

[6] Sayce, *loc. cit.*, p. 284, quoting W. A. I., IV, 70, 55; II, 59, 5.

[7] *Ibid.*, p. 285–6; quoting W. A. I., IV, 28, 3.

[8] Even Pliny, *Nat. Hist.*, VIII, ch. 89, enumerates among Capræ the roebuck, the chamois, the goat, and the antelope-oryx. The Roman offering of the "Cervaria Ovis," in which the sheep was made to pass for a stag, shows the close connection existing between these animals in the minds of the ancients.

[9] VII, 20.

Southern Arabia, in connection with Athtar worship ; at Mecca, probably in connection with the worship of Al-Ozza : and in Phœnicia,
both on gems and on coins of Laodicea ad Mare. An annual sacrifice
of a stag took place at the latter place on the Phœnician coast, which
was looked upon as a substitute for a more ancient sacrifice of a
maiden, offered to a goddess whom Porphyry [1] calls Athene, whilst
Pausanias [2] identifies her with Brauronian Artemis, supposing her
cultus to have been introduced by Seleucus. Mr. Robertson Smith,[3]
from whom I have borrowed these details, has, however, pointed out
that the town [4] is much older than its re-christening by Seleucus, and
that, if the goddess had been Greek, she would not have been identified with both Athene and Artemis. He regards her, in fact, as a
form of Astarte, the ancient Tyche of the city.

Among the Greeks, deer were held sacred to Apollo at Delphi.[5]
One of the most important among the archaic statues of the god—
that executed by Kanakhos—which stood in the temple of Didymus,
near Miletus (about VIth century B. C.), if we believe Pliny,[6] represented the god holding his bow and carrying a young deer upon his
outstretched hand.

Deer and stags were also sacred to Artemis,[7] and the famous statue
of this goddess in the Louvre [8]—which represents her, according to the
conception of the artists of the IVth century B. C., dressed with the
short chiton—shows her accompanied by the deer, her common attend-
ant. A number of statuettes of Artemis-Kybele, with the deer or with
the dog, were found by Dr. Richter at Achna, Cyprus.[9] Moreover, on
many monuments, she wears the *nebris*,[10] or fawn-skin, over her chiton.

---

[1] *De Abst.*, II, 56.

[2] III, 16-8.

[3] *Religion of the Semites*, p. 447, 1889.

[4] Ramitha in Phoen, acc. to Philo ap. Steph. Byz., quoted by Mr. Robertson
Smith, *loc. cit.*

[5] O. Keller, *Thiere des classischen Alterthums in Culturhistorischer Beziehung*, pp.
90-93.

[6] Pliny, XXXIV, 19. The description is obscure ; in this I have followed Collignon's interpretation.

[7] Comp. Callimachus' *Hymn to Artemis*.

[8] M. Collignon, *Mythologie Figurée de la Grèce*, p. 107. Compare the Corinthian
Puteal as given by Mr. A. Michaelis in *Journ. of Hellenic Studies*, vol. VI, p. 48, on
which Artemis is also represented with the deer which she holds by the fore-leg.

[9] *Ancient Places of Worship in Kypros*, p. 37, pl. iv.

[10] The nebris, or fawn-skin, and the ægis, or goat-skin, were associated with the gods
in Greek mythology. The latter seems to have been regarded as possessed of divine
or magic virtues. See Homer, *Iliad*, v, 738 ; xviii, 204 ; xv, 229, 307, 321 ; xxiv, 30.

Cervidæ were also sacred to Aphrodite.[1] Indeed, the worship of the Greek Artemis seems, in early times, to have been very much confused with that of female divinities whose attributes had little or nothing in common with the severe type of the stern goddess. And, difficult as it is to understand how the later Greeks could recognize the chaste sister of Apollo in such deities as the Persian and the Ephesian Artemis, we have already seen that, as a matter of fact, Astarte was identified by ancient writers, not only with Artemis, but also with Athene. Artemis was originally an Eastern deity ; and Mr. Cecil Smith, in pointing out how frequently she figures on vases decorated with the " Oriental " design,[2] has only strengthened the evidence.

The recent discoveries of Dr. M. Ohnefalsch-Richter in Cyprus also tend to confirm the view[3] which sees in the different Greek goddesses mere aspects of the great Nature-Mother : In the archaic art of Cyprus, the same form—borrowed from that of Nana-Ishtar—was made use of by the Cyprian artists to represent Ashtoret-Aphrodite, and Tanit-Artemis-Kybele. Later on, however, the former divinity appears as a nude female form, pressing her hands to her breasts, whilst the latter continues to be draped.[4]

Shrines have been brought to light by the same careful explorer— belonging to about the same period as those from which our potsherds have been derived—in which Artemis-Kybele,[5] Aphrodite-Kybele,[6] Anat-Athene,[7] and Astarte-Aphrodite were respectively worshipped ; and Dr. Richter's conclusions, drawn from such facts, derive these various forms from one original type, for which he claims an Asiatic genesis.[8]

The Ægis of Zeus (the word here used in the sense of shield) was made of the skin of the goat Amaltheia, whose milk was supposed to have nourished the infant god. Athene and Apollo are stated to have borrowed it from Zeus ; see *Iliad*, xv, 229, 307, 318, 360: xxiv, 20; ii, 447, 449; xviii, 204; xxi, 400. (Comp. Smith's *Dict. of Greek and Roman Antiq.*, p. 34, 1891.) The nebris is also associated with Dionysus and his orgiastic *cortège* (*Ibid.*, p. 225).

[1] O. Keller, *loc. cit.*, p. 94, says that it was also sacred to Athene, and, at Phocis, to Isis (*loc. cit.*, p. 96). Compare Callimachus' *Hymn to Artemis*, v, 386, where Athene is said to have formed the flute of the bones of the deer.

[2] *Journ. of Hell. Studies*, vol. V, p. 237, on " Four Archaic Vases from Rhodes."

[3] E. Curtius, *Die griechische Götterlehre vom geschichtlichen Standpunkte*, 1875.

[4] Dr. Max Ohnefalsch-Richter, *Ancient Places of Worship in Kypros*, p. 42, pl. xi, 1891.

[5] *Ibid.*, p. 11.

[6] *Ibid.*, p. 12.

[7] *Ibid.*, pp. 15, 16, 23.

[8] *Ibid.*, pp. 30-32.

Apollo and Aphrodite seem to have been the most important divinities of Naukratis, and this reminds us that in the region of Paphos (Cyprus), Apollo occupied a conspicuous position by the side of the same goddess.[1]

The special association of the cervidæ with the worship of Apollo and with that of Aphrodite makes it likely that the frequent recurrence of these animals upon the Naukratis vases is not a purely fortuitous circumstance. And the fact that the sherds so decorated were found in the temene of Apollo and of Aphrodite—where they had originally been brought by the faithful as offerings—lends some support to the view expressed by Mr. Goodyear[2] that the decoration on these vases was symbolical. It is, at least, probable that it was selected, either by the artist himself or by the devout purchaser, with a view to religious symbolism, and as particularly appropriate to the end for which these vessels were destined.

Among the other mythological animals that are frequently represented upon the painted incised vases of Naukratis, is the boar—and as this animal is seldom, if ever, found as a symbolical decorative object among the antiquities of Mesopotamia[3] which are contemporaneous with the use of this "serial" design, its presence here deserves, perhaps, more than a passing mention.

The pig, in the pre-Semitic religion of Chaldæa, was sacred to the war-god Adar, or Ninib,[4] who was originally the sun-god of Nipur,[5] and was regarded as the offspring of the great local tutelary divinity, Mullil, the ruler of the under-world and of the dead.[6] Although a

---

[1] Ibid., p. 23.

[2] Grammar of the Lotus.

[3] As far as I know, pigs do not occur in the symbolical art of Assyria, where it was not a sacrificial animal. There is, however, a representation of a pig on a clay tablet from Babylon, reproduced by Mr. Babelon in Manual of Oriental Antiq., p. 123. 1889.

[4] Sayce, loc. cit., p. 153. The "Lord of the Asu." According to Jensen, Kosmogonie der Babyl., the Asu of the woods is the wild boar.

[5] Sayce, loc. cit., p. 152, quoting W. A. I., II, 57, 51, 76: There is among the objects exhumed from the mound of Niffer, ancient Nipur, by the "Peters Expedition," which are now in the Museum of Archæology and Palæontology of the University of Pennsylvania, a fine clay representation of a pig. This specimen is a bas-relief about three inches long, of poorly-baked clay, but the animal is beautifully drawn, and modelled with a great deal of expression. It is an object complete in itself, and must have been used either as a votive offering or an image. It presents an archaic appearance, crumbles easily, and the clay, wherever it is broken off, exhibits the unbaked blue core.

[6] Sayce, loc. cit., pp. 145, 146, etc.

solar god, Ninib was, therefore associated with darkness and death, and Mr. Jensen,[1] quoting a hymn in which the god is addressed as the "light of Heaven and earth illuminating the interior of the Underworld," describes him as the East Sun, *before* it rises. He is also the "merciful one, who gives life, who causes the dead to live."[2]

He was called "Lord of the Swine," a title which, according to Mr. Sayce,[3] would appear to have been dropped and lost during the Semitic period of Mesopotamian history; at least, it does not occur in the later texts.

Wild boar's meat was forbidden food on the banks of the Euphrates, in the months of Ab and of Marshesvan;[4] and the very mention of the domestic pig is said to have been avoided in the Semitic-Babylonian and Assyrian inscriptions.[5]

Ramman,[6] the god of the luminous air, regarded in the later mythology as the husband of Ishtar, whose earlier consort was Tammuz, the sun-god of Eridu—when worshipped as Mâtu (Martu), the lord of the tempest, minister of Bel—was, it would seem, known as "Khummuntsir," an Akkadized form of the Semitic "Khumtsiru"—a pig.[7] As Bel of Nipur is the Semitic form of the ancient Akkadian divinity, Mullil,[8] Ramman, in this aspect, may be regarded as the equivalent of Ninib.

Complicated as are these myths, it seems evident that the animal

---

[1] *Kosmogonie der Babyl.*, p. 475.

[2] Jensen, *loc. cit.*, p. 471, quoting K. 128.

[3] *Loc. cit.*, p. 153. In K. 161, 1–8, quoted by Mr. Sayce, one of the remedies prescribed for heart disease is "swine's flesh."

[4] I am indebted to Dr. Morris Jastrow for the information that the latter month is designated by an ideogram which, in II R., 57, 32, is a title of Ninib, whilst the chief ideographic element of the written name of "Ab" means "fire," and according to a passage in the inscription of Sargon, Cyl. 61, Ab is the month sacred to the fire-god, who is, of course, brought into direct connection with the sun-god.

[5] Sayce, *loc. cit.*, p. 83.

[6] Sayce, *loc. cit.*, p. 212, identifies this god with the Syrian sun-god Rimmon (Zech. xii, 11) whose untimely death was mourned in the valley of Megiddo by the plain of Yezreel every year, just as the death of Tammuz was mourned by the women of Phœnicia and of Jerusalem (Ezech. viii, 14), or as Adonis was mourned by Aphrodite (comp. *loc. cit.*, p. 227).

[7] According to Prof. Robertson Smith, *Religion of the Semites*, p. 201, swine's flesh was forbidden to all the Semites, and that animal was only sacrificed in certain exceptional rites on certain solemn occasions. The same author expresses a doubt (*loc. cit.*, p. 143) as to whether swine's flesh was "taboo" by the Semites because it was regarded as holy or as impure.

[8] Sayce, *loc. cit.*, p. 103.

we are now considering was connected with the sun-god in the early religion of Chaldæa; but with the sun-god in its fiercer and darker aspects, anthropomorphized as the warlike son of the lord of the under-world.

Mr. Sayce [1] suggests that the Semitic abhorrence of the swine may have caused it to be used to symbolize the ancient rivalry of the sun-god of Nipur and of the sun-god of Eridu; but, as we find that the swine-myth underwent a similar process in other religious systems, a purely local explanation of the phenomenon which turned this animal into the adversary of the divine type that he had once personified seems in-sufficient, and it is much more likely that the swine, after having been associated with the sun in the underworld—i. e., with the sun which, dying, is born again and brings with it all life and fertility, came, in the course of time, to represent the darkness that swallows or de-stroys the light and life-giving god, and thus assumed the part of his antagonist.

This seems to be the only way in which we can account for the con-tradictory position occupied in various mythologies by the swine.

Among the Egyptians, there is reason to believe that, in early times, this animal was not regarded with the aversion which it inspired later, probably under Semitic influence. It may be seen among the flocks of Amten, a high functionary of Pyramid times; [2] and, at that period, that animal was used along with others, in hieroglyphic writing, as the deter-minative for " herd." [3] The fact that the sow was sacred to Isis [4] also lends support to this view. The hippopotamus, an animal which seems to have been classed by the Egyptians with the swine, [5] was a favorite form of the mother-goddess, who in her name of Ta-urt, typified fertility; and who, although mythologically regarded as the consort of Set, [6] the brother and opponent of Osiris, was mentioned in the legend as having assisted Isis to bring forth Horos.

As the *mother of the gods*, Apet, who at Thebes in Ptolemaic times was held in highest veneration, [7] was represented under the form of a

---

[1] Sayce, *loc. cit.*, p. 236.

[2] Lepsius, *Denk.* ii, 5.

[3] Chabas, *Études sur l'Antiq. Historiq.*, p. 407.

[4] On sow-amulets is often inscribed the wish " that Isis may grant happiness to the owner of this sow." Maspero, *Catalog. de Bulaq.*, No. 4158. 1883.

[5] Lefébure, *Les Yeux d'Horus*, p. 54.

[6] The destructive power of the earth, who also typifies darkness as opposed to light. His connection with the earth is shown by the fact that the determinative of his name is a stone.

[7] Mr. de la Rochemonteix, *Rec. de Travaux*. Vol. III, pp. 73, etc., *Le Temple*

hippopotamus. In a papyrus in the Louvre collection,[1] in which the different attributes of the divine power are symbolized under various animal forms, the sow represents fertility and motherhood;[2] and the mother of Min, the mummiform generative god, was represented under the shape of a white sow.[3]

In the Todtenbuch, the swine seems to be more particularly connected with El-Kab, the ancient city of the South, whose vulture goddess, Nekheb, had from time immemorial typified Upper Egypt. In the chapter cxii, which bears some relation to this locality, the swine appears in the *rôle* of the adversary of light ; and much more than an allusion is made[4] to the danger with which "the eye of Horos" was threatened at the hands of Set, metamorphosed as a black swine—the solar nature of the "eye of Horos" being made clear by the further remark that "its might burnt the black swine."[5]

The same chapter[6] also records the fact that oxen, gazelles, and swine were ordered by Horos to be sacrificed to the gods, the latter animal having been declared abominable by the sun-god Ra.[7] Set is often mentioned in the texts as having swallowed the eye of Horos,[8] or as having been compelled to throw up that which he had eaten,[9] and according to Chabas,[10] swine are frequently referred to as odious to Horos.

The classics also allude to the mythological character of the pig as the antagonist of Osiris. Plutarch,[11] for instance, relates that Typhon found the chest containing the body of Osiris whilst pursuing a sow

d'Apet. See also Wiedemann, *Die Religion des alten Ägyptens,* p. 88–89, where the syncretism of the mother-goddesses into this type is discussed.

[1] No. 3148.

[2] Paul Pierret, *Le Panthéon Égyptien,* p. 37.

[3] Stèle de Metternich, Reinisch, *Monuments de Miramar,* 117.

[4] *Todt.,* chap. cxii, pp. 3, 4, 5.

[5] In a papyrus of Leyden, studied by Chabas, and which contains an incantation, it is stated that, from the burnt hind quarters of the "Sow of the Sun," there comes a fat that ascends to heaven and falls back upon earth in the shape of asps.—Lefébure, *Les Yeux d'Horus,* p. 58.

[6] *Ibid.,* chap. cxii, p. 6. Plutarch, *Is. and Osiris,* 31, says that only animals disagreeable to the gods were sacrificed.

[7] Comp. Herod, ii, 47, who says that swine were regarded as so unclean that the Egyptians washed in the river, without undressing, any one whom a pig had touched. Swineherds were regarded as unclean and compelled to intermarry.

[8] For instance, *Todt.,* cxvi, p. 1. *Denk.,* iv, pl. 46, p. 1.

[9] *Todt.,* chap. cviii, p. v.

[10] *Études sur l'Antiquité Historique,* pp. 404–5.

[11] *De Is. et Os.,* 18–42.

in the moonlight This is obviously a corrupt version of the myth, for both he and Herodotos [1] state that pigs were sacrificed to the god and eaten once a year at the time of the full moon ; and that this celebration took place all over Egypt at the same time—*i. c.*, on the eve of the feast of Osiris, on the day of the Great Lamentations of Isis and Nephthys.[2] Chabas[3] mentions the sacrifice of a pig as taking place at Medinet Abu at that time, the 25th of Choiak.

According to Egyptian texts, the great festival in honor of Osiris took place in Egypt at the time of the winter solstice, when the days are shortest ; and they culminated after seven days of mourning for the death of the god. These occurred on the 24th Choiak. From the 12th to the 24th, elaborate preparations, prescribed by regulations, were made in the temples. Figures of Osiris were made of dough mixed with spices, aromatic woods, gold, silver, and even precious stones, all cast in a mould, and set to dry in the setting sun, embalmed and placed in a coffin.

At the appointed time these were taken in solemn procession on the Nile, at night, accompanied by the other gods, in 34 barks, illuminated by 365 lamps. After this the images lay in state in the temples for seven days, and were then buried in great pomp.[4]

In the island of Cyprus, swine were sacrificed piacularly from ancient times in connection with the worship of Adonis and Aphrodite, and wild boars were offered on April 2d. Mr. Robertson Smith[5] gives it as his opinion that this rite was originally intended to repre-

---

[1] ii, 47. He says to the moon and Dionysos (*i. c.*, Osiris), and adds that on the eve of the festival of the god, every Egyptian sacrificed a hog in front of his house, and that the poor people, who could not afford to do this, formed figures of pigs out of dough, which they offered after baking them.

Although the Egyptian myth in which the pig plays a part is obviously a solar myth, the lunar element which appears to be associated with it in the narratives of Herodotos and Plutarch is further brought to our attention in a papyrus quoted by Mr. Lefébure (*Les Yeux d'Horus*, p. 52), in which the lunar god *Thoth* is represented armed with two knives and striking at a pig, whilst another vignette shows Horos, the sun-god, attacking seven swine.

[2] De Horrack, *Les Lamentations d'Isis et de Nephthys*, pl. i, p. iv, f. 3. Quoted by Lefébure, *Les Yeux d'Horus*, p. 48.

[3] *Loc. cit.*

[4] For details of these important "*mysteries*," see V. Loret *Les Fêtes d'Osiris au Mois de Choiak. Recueil de Travaux*, vol. iii, pp. 43–57 ; vol. iv, pp. 21, etc. ; vol. v, pp. 85, etc. This celebration of the death of Osiris was followed by that of the new birth of the god.

[5] *Loc. cit.*, p. 392.

sent the death of the swine-god Adonis, and was not in its primitive
form an act of vengeance for his death.

On the other hand, the warlike character of the sun-god of Nipur,
"lord of the swine," reminds us of the Ares of Greek mythology,
who, under the shape of the wild boar, slew the beautiful lover of
Aphrodite.

According to ancient writers,[1] swine were, therefore, held especially
sacred to Astarte and Aphrodite by the Syrians.   Occasional sacrifices of swine were offered to the latter goddess at Argos[2] and in
Thessaly,[3] but Prof. Robertson Smith[4] regards the Semitic origin of
these as less clear than that of the rites connected with the Cyprian
goddess.

The animal is a familiar figure in Greek legend, where it also plays
the part of a god-sent scourge.   The killing of the boar of Eryman-
thus is among the labors of the solar hero Herakles, and the exploits
of Theseus against the boar of Crommyon, as well as those of Meleager
against the Calydonian boar, sent as a scourge by Artemis, are too
familiar to need dwelling upon.

It is certainly a fact that the pig played an important part in the
sacrificial rites of the Greeks[5] and of the Romans.   Swine were numbered among the sacred herds of the Greek temples,[6] and, according
to Preller,[7] pigs were sacrificed to Herakles.   We have already seen
that they were also sacrificed to Aphrodite.   But it is especially to
Demeter, the earth-goddess, who presided over the fertility of nature
and the fruitfulness of human marriage, that pigs were consecrated by
the Greeks.[8]

---

[1] Lucian *Dea Syria*, liv; and Antiphanus ap. Athen., iii, 49.

[2] Athen., iii, 49.

[3] Straton, ix, 5–17.   In other localities, where no doubt a totemistic element survived, the sacrifice of swine to Aphrodite was specifically prohibited.   See Smith's
Greek and Roman Antiquities, vol. ii, p. 582.

[4] *Loc. cit.*

[5] In Greece the pig was the great purificatory sacrifice, whilst among the Semites
the offering of this animal was connected with mystic rites, and was not an ordinary
piaculum.   See Robertson Smith, *loc. cit.*, 456.

[6] On an inscription containing a list of regulations concerning the enclosure of the
temple of Athena Alea, discovered in Arcadia by Mr. Fougères and published by Mr.
Bérard in *Bull. de la Correspondance Hellén.*, April, 1889, certain rules and fines are
mentioned with respect to the "sacred herds," among which swine are numbered.

[7] *Griechisch. Myth.*, i, 303.

[8] Acc. to Herod. (v. 57, 61), the worship of Demeter was introduced into Attica by
the Gephyreans, who stated that they came from Eretria, but whom Herodotos re-

In the Thesmophoria, a festival celebrated at seed-time in Athens, as well as in other places, pigs were sacrificed. And a scholion on Lucian's *Dialogues of Courtesans*, a translation of which is given by Mr. Andrew Lang in his interesting article on "Demeter and the Pig,"[1] tells how pigs were then thrown into "the caverns" of Demeter and Persephone,[2] and how the women went down into these recesses to fetch the remains of the victims, which they placed upon the altars." "And it is believed," says the scholion, "that whoever takes of this flesh and mixes it with the seed corn will have the richest harvest and abundance."[3]

After doing this they deposited there the "well-known images." These rites were called : "The carrying of things not to be spoken, and they are performed in the way for the fruitfulness of the fields and of human kind."[4]

Sir Charles Newton, in his excavations at Cnidos, on the site of the temenos of Demeter, discovered the crypts of the temple, in which were found certain small figures of pigs in marble, and at the very bottom the bones of swine and other animals.[5]

Votive offerings to Demeter are found, consisting of pigs, bearing children on their backs—probably brought to the shrine of the mother-goddess by wedded women anxious for offspring.

The pig was a common purificatory offering,[6] and in the usual representations of Demeter she accordingly appears accompanied by a pig and a purificatory torch.[7] In the Eleusinian Mysteries the initiated bathed in the sea, each with the pig intended as an offering to

---

garded as Phoenicians. He also states that the worship of Demeter was originally derived from the Isis-worship of the Egyptians (ii, 59. 122, 123, 155), and that the Thesmophoria were introduced in the same manner (ii, 171).

[1] *Nineteenth Century*, 1887, vol. xxi, p. 559.

[2] Comp. Pausanias (viii, 25-4), who says that at Thelpusa, in Arcadia, there was a hole, sacred to Demeter Erinys, into which live pigs were cast, and that in Boeotia the people used to throw young pigs into crypts (*loc. cit.*, ix, 8-1).

[3] Acc. to Mr. Frazer (*The Golden Bough*, ii, p. 49), in Hessen and Meiningen pigs are eaten on Ash Wednesday or Candlemas, and the bones are kept until sowing time, when they are put into the field, sown or mixed with the seed in the bag. This is supposed to make the flax grow well (comp. *loc. cit.*, p. 29). Comp. E. Hugo Meyer, *Germanische Mythol*, p. 103, who, in addition to these facts, states that farmers stick a pig's tail into the ground at sowing-time ; and that brides were presented with a pig's tail on their wedding-day.

[4] Mr. A. Lang, *loc. cit.*, p. 562.

[5] Sir Charles Newton, *Halicarnassus*, pp. 383, 391, 422. cf. plate viii.

[6] Æschy., *Eumenides*, 283.

[7] Smith's *Dict. of Greek and Roman Antiq.*, ii, 833, 1891.

the goddess,[1] and each sacrificed a pig on the 17th of Boedromion— *i. e.*, the day of the great Eleusinia. There is little doubt that every family did the same at Athens.

Mr. Frazer[2] suggests that the pig which, later, was sacrificed to Demeter, was originally the goddess in animal form. This seems very probable, and it is likely, as remarked by Mr. Lang, that the fecundity of the animal, joined with its habit of rooting up the earth, may have primitively led to its association with the under-world and its rulers.

According to Livy in the rites of the Roman fetiales—rites which may possibly go back to a time when stone implements were still in use among the ancestors of the ancient inhabitants of Italy[3]—the victim slain by the pater patratus with the sacred flint preserved for the purpose in the temple of Jupiter Feretrius, to consecrate the solemn oath sworn by the Roman people, was a hog.[4]

This animal was, moreover, held especially sacred to the Lares,[5] and the sow was closely connected with their worship as well as with that of the Manes.[6] In the Cerialia, a spring festival celebrated at Rome

---

[1] Plutarch, *Phocion*, xxviii, quot. by Mr. Lang, *loc. cit.*

A pregnant sow was offered to Demeter at Mykonos and Andania.

[2] *Loc. cit.*

[3] E. B. Tylor. *Researches into the Early Hist. of Mankind*, p. 226.

[4] Livy, i, 24; xxx, 43. " If by public counsel or by wicked fraud they swerve first, in that day, O Jove, smite thou the Roman people as I here to-day shall smite this hog ; and smite them so much more, as thou art abler and stronger," and having said this he struck the hog with a flint-stone.

[5] On an ancient altar, dated in the ninth year of Augustus, and dedicated to the Lares Augusti, which was exhumed in Rome on the banks of the Tiber, near the little church of San Bartolomeo de' Vaccinari, there is a bas-relief representing four " Magistri " about to accomplish the rites of their cultus and to sacrifice a bull—the animal more particularly identified with the genius of Augustus, and a hog, the special offering to the Lares. See *Revue de l'Hist. des Religions*, Vol. XX, p. 39-40. *Bull. Arch. de la Religion Romaine*, by George Lafaye.

The pig also appears associated with the bull and with the sheep in the ancient purificatory rite of the " Suovetaurilia," which was in its origin dedicated to Mars in his primitive agricultural aspect ; and which, with the development of this deity into a war-god, was afterward applied to warlike purposes.

[6] *Tibul.*, i, 10, 26. " Placaris . . . Lares avidaque porca," Hor. Od., iii, 23, 4 ; " Immolet . . . porcum Laribus," Sat., ii, 3, 164 ; Prop., iv, i, 23 : " Parva saginati lustrabant compita porci," in honor of the Lares compitales. Compare J. A. Hild, *La Légende d'Enée*, in *Revue de l'Hist. des Religious*, vi, p. 151, etc.

In the legend of Lavinium, the sow, escaping from the knife of the sacrificing priest, marks the spot where the town shall be built, and according to Varro (*Re Rustica*, ii, 4, 18), quoted by Mr. Hild, *loc. cit.*, p. 165, a brazen image of the thirty

in honor of Ceres, and intended to commemorate the return of Pro-
serpina to earth, no bloody sacrifice was permitted save that of a
sow.[1] According to Macrobius,[2] a sow or a ewe lamb was
offered to Juno-Lucina on the calends of every month, and there
seems to be good reason[3] for connecting these rites with those which
were celebrated in Cyprus in honor of Aphrodite, to whom, as we have
already seen, both the goat and the pig were sacrificed.

We, therefore, find the pig here also connected with death and with
life, with the fecundity of motherhood and with the darkness of the
grave, and among other Aryan peoples the hog, as well as the wild
boar, is a disguise for the sun in the night or in the darkness of the
clouds.[4]

Many legends, fairy-tales, and ancient customs preserved in Europe
betray the ideas which, in the symbolism of the Aryan races, were once
attached to the swine. Among them it represented fat and plenty.

According to Mr. E. Hugo Meyer, the pig is one of the oldest as

---

small pigs mentioned in Æn. viii, 43, 81, was set in the public place, and the body
of the sow herself was preserved in brine.

[1] *Ibid.* Fast. iv, 414.

[2] i, 15, 19.

[3] See Prof. Robertson Smith, *loc. cit.*, p. 453.

[4] Gubernatis, *Zoological Mythology*, ii, p. 6.

In the Rig-Veda (i, 114–5; I am indebted for the following passage to Prof. E.
W. Hopkins) the sun is invoked as "the wild boar of the sky, red, with braided hair,
swift, beauty(ful), we reverently call upon, carrying in his hands the best medicines.
May he grant us protection, shelter, and guard." In the Puranas (Gubernatis, *loc. cit.*,
ii, p. 8) the third avatar of Vishnu is the wild boar; and a transparent myth given at
length by Burnouf (*L'Inde Française*) tells how the sun-god Vishnu, transforming himself into a wild boar, pierced through the earth and penetrated to the infernal regions,
where he saw the feet of Mahadeva. On his return he was saluted the first-born of the
gods. Yet the same contradiction which exists in other mythologies and associates
the swine with darkness, the enemy of light, may also be detected here, and a passage of the Rig-Veda (i, 61, 6. Comp. v, x, 99—6) shows us the god, killing the
monster wild boar who steals that which is destined for the gods, with the weapon
stolen from the celestial blacksmith Tvashtar. According to Mr. Gubernatis, in the
Hindu mythology, where the storm plays so important a part, the boar is not only
connected with light and fertility in their struggle against the darkness of night or
of winter, but we also find it associated with light and fertility in their contest with
the darkness of the storm-cloud. Indra himself takes here the form of the boar
(Gubernatis, *loc. cit.*, ii, p. 8).

In the Avesta (*Yast* x, 70, etc.) this animal is the embodiment of Verethraghna,
who, as such, is there associated with Mithra, before whom he runs "wrathful" and
"death-dealing" to his foes. Comp. x, 127, where it is said that "behind him
drives Atar all-ablaze"; and the awful kingly glory.

well as the principal sacrificial animal among the Teutonic peoples—who reared it for the purpose, and ate it in all solemnity at stated times. It was sacrificed to Freyr,[1] at the Yule-feast, at which time offerings were made to insure the fertility of the soil.

On the Lower Rhine, the "St. Anthony's parish swine"[2] was distributed and eaten on January 17th; and similar solemn sacrifices of the pig took place at various dates in different places—which were connected either with the beginning of winter, or with harvest-time. A pig of dough was offered at Christmas-time; and this rite was performed in the same intention as that practiced in the North—and according to which the Yule-tide male and female goats were baked and mixed with the seed-grain when sown.[3] We have already seen that such rites were common in antiquity,[4] and that, in these substitutes, was concealed a "mystery."

Their meaning is abundantly explained by the customs which, as already noted, are preserved in Meiningen; where the picked bones of the sacrificial hog are mixed and sown with the seed-grain. We have seen, where dealing with the worship of Demeter, what were the ideas that inspired the rites of which these customs are a survival.

In Germany, as formerly in England, the custom of serving an ornamented boar's head at dinner on Christmas day is, very likely, a survival of the ancient rite celebrated at the time of the winter solstice, when the boar was sacrificed to the god who—descending then into the underworld—was to return again, bringing life, fertility, and plenty to the world. And there are legends too numerous to find place here, which are more or less closely connected with the ancient myth, and in which the tusk of the boar appears as life-giving in the morning and as death-dealing in the evening.[5]

[1] The Spring Sun-God. See E. H. Meyer, *Germanische Mythologe.*, p. 103. This author, however, regards the swine-myth as purely a storm myth.

[2] "St. Antoniusgemeindeschwein," *loc. cit.* I am told that, in some parts of Russia each village sacrifices a hog to the House-spirit, or Jar, on March 25th. This is divided among the villagers, and every man forthwith buries his piece under his door-step. This insures prosperity and plenty. After this the ceremonies of the "Death-week" take place. These culminate after several days in the driving out of death—who is finally drowned under the shape of a hideous dummy.

[3] E. H. Meyer, *loc. cit.*, p. 103.

[4] The "Kavanim" which, according to Jeremiah (vii, 18), the women of Judah and of Jerusalem made of kneaded dough, and which they dedicated to the "Queen of Heaven," were either, like the figures of Osiris (see above, p. 111), images used in the worship of Tammuz, or substitutes for living offerings.

[5] Gubernatis, *loc. cit.*, ii. pp. 14-16.

Although the Eddas may appear of too recent origin to be of any very decisive value in the interpretation of mythical ideas that seem to reach back to the very dawn of religious thought, it is interesting to note how very clearly they explain the notion which lies at the foundation of the antithesis in which the swine plays a double *rôle* as a solar symbol, and at the same time as a funereal offering associated with the under-world, and regarded not only as suitable food for the Manes, but as the embodiment of ever-renewed life.

They show us the boar with "golden bristles," the "boar of war," representing the sun, "*glowing in Walhalla*,"[1] and it is upon its substance that the souls of the immortal heroes feed to all eternity,[2] for its life was ever renewed.[3] In their mythology the boar was especially sacred to Freyr, and to his sister Freyja. The latter was a nature-goddess, and was closely associated with her brother in his character of the "sun regenerated in the spring." The golden boar, the symbol of the sun, is therefore connected with her, as well as with Freyr.[4]

The ideas embodied in the symbolism of the swine, as it appears in the Eddas, bring us back, therefore—at the end of the journey through space and time, which we have undertaken in pursuit of the pig—to our original starting-point; that is, to very nearly the same stage of the myth as we found existing in pre-Semitic Chaldæa—where we saw the

---

[1] I am indebted to Dr. Hermann Collitz for the following passages bearing upon the subject, which he has had the kindness to collect for me: *Song of Hyndla, Older Edda*, cf. *Corpus Poeticum Boreale*, vol. i, p. 226, 19: "Thou seemest to dream! to say that I have my lover with me on the journey to Walhall, where the swine Gullinbursti [*i. e.*, golden bristle] glows; Hildisvini [*i. e.*, the boar of war] which the skillful dwarfs Dain and Nabbi wrought for me."

[2] *Grimnismal, Older Edda*, cf. *Corpus Poeticum Boreale*, i, p. 75, 18: "Andhrimnir [*i. e.*, Breath-Sooty] cooks Saehrimnir [*i. e.*, Sea-Sooty, the hog], in Eldhrimnir [*i. e.*, Fire-Sooty, the kettle], the best of bacon; but few know what the Einherjar [*i. e.*, Host of the Chosen] live on." This extremely obscure passage receives elucidation from another in the later Edda, which evidently refers to it: "Gylfaginning, c, 39:" ". . . . Never is the crowd in Walhall so great that the meat of the boar whose name is Saehrimnir was not sufficient. This one is cooked every day, and every night it is whole again." Then the above-quoted passage of the older Edda is given. At the funeral burning of Baldur and his wife Nanna, many guests were present: "Odin and Frigg, and the Valkyrjur, and Odin's ravens and Freyr, the sun-god, drove in his car, dragged by his boar, whose name was Gullinbursti (or Slidrugtanni). Heimdall rode on his stallion Gulltopp, and Freyja drove with her cats."

[3] The boar eaten every day by the Einherjar—i. e., the heroes in Walhall—and reviving every night, is an image of the sun. (Simrock, *Deutsche Mythol.*, 5th ed., p. 188.)

[4] Mogk, *Teutonic Mythol.*, in Paul's *Grundriss*, i, p. 1109.

swine-god in the underworld, *i. e.*, the type of light, concealed in darkness—worshipped as the giver of life, born of death.

From the above it would seem that the swine had been very generally associated by primitive men in the early stages of their religious evolution, with mother-earth and the Chthonian powers ruling the underworld. With the development of solar worship, which properly belongs to the period when man passed from the pastoral to the agricultural age, and with the recognized influence of the sun upon the fecundity of the earth, the swine was taken as a symbol of the sun beneath the horizon, issuing forth from the night, and it thus became particularly associated with the male element in the return of light, of life, and óf fertility. It is evidently a later outgrowth of the myth that made of him the type of the darkness of winter, or of the storm, which overcomes the radiance and power of the sun ; and that, by a process common in mythology, caused it to personify the adversary of the god, one of the aspects of which it had once been used to symbolize.

If we keep in view the Asiatic origin of Aphrodite, her close connection with the mother-goddesses of Cyprus and Asia, and the myths which connect her with the vernal sun-god, lord of the swine, killed to be born again, it is easy to understand the important position which the animal we are considering occupied in her worship; and why it should occur as a favorite theme upon the decoration of the vases recovered at Naukratis, where that goddess was evidently held in high veneration.

Indeed, rare as is the swine in the later symbolical decorative art of Mesopotamia, it is a form commonly used not only by the Greek artists of the Delta, but by those of Greece and of the Mediterranean basin who constantly introduce it among the animals composing the original series in the " Oriental " design, as it appears in Assyria, whence, carried by commerce, it found its way at least as far as Etruria.

There is in the " Lamborn Collection " now deposited in the Pennsylvania Museum and School of Industrial Art, in Philadelphia, a large shallow bowl of very coarse red unglazed ware, the rim of which is decorated with series of animals stamped in low-relief, whose attitudes and general expression are very similar to those on our sherds. Among them is one which I take to be a boar. I am indebted to the kindness of the owner, Dr. Robert H. Lamborn, for the information that he was induced to purchase this bowl in Rome some years ago, because of its close resemblance to similar specimens forming part of the sepulchral furniture of the Campana tomb at Veii. As the interments in this locality are considered earlier than 400 B. C., it is interesting to find that our design had become sufficiently common to be adapted to and stamped upon such coarse ware, not later than the fifth century B. C. We have already seen that it occurs on a bronze figure found in the Polledrara tomb; and another example may be seen, applied as a border, in the incised decoration of a fine bronze cista from Palestrina (ancient Prœnesta), now in the British Museum.[1] On this the boar appears between a lion and a leopard—the latter is attacking him from behind; and the attitudes of the animals are strongly suggestive of the scenes depicted on the Assyrian patera reproduced above (fig. 39).

After what has been said above with regard to the worship of Kybele in Cyprus, and of the various foreign types which Dr. Richter discovered there, as it were, in process of formation, one need not wonder at finding the Phrygian lion—the animal sacred to the great Phrygian mother-goddess, "Matar Kubile,"[2] used as a favorite theme upon the painted vases of Naukratis in the sixth century B. C.[3]

The accompanying potsherd (fig. 40) is only one of many examples,

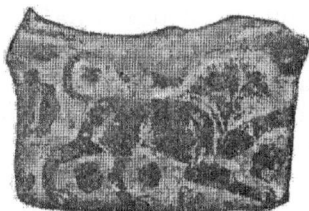

Fig. 40.   Potsherd from Naukratis in the Museum of the University of Pennsylvania.

some of which reproduce the well-known group which is familiar to us from the gateway of the Acropolis of Mykenae—two lions facing each other—that is, the typical heraldic motive commonly met with on the tombs of Phrygia, and through which if, as is probable, Mr. W. M. Ramsay[4] is correct in his interpretation of the Phrygian ideas as to the hereafter, the sepulchral monument became a shrine dedicated to the mother-goddess.

These few fragments of broken pottery show us the Mediterranean region in the light of a huge intellectual churn into which the most

---

[1] Murray, *loc. cit.*, p. 143, fig. 57.

[2] W. M. Ramsay. *Sepulchral Customs in Ancient Phrygia. Journ. Hell. Studies.* v, p. 246.

[3] *Loc. cit.*, pp. 254, etc.

[4] *Loc. cit.*, pp. 254, etc.

heterogenous elements were thrown, not alone by conquest, but more particularly by peaceful traffic; and out of which sprang many of those decorative forms which the Greeks idealized and handed down to us.

That such commercial activity had its origin in the far-distant past there could be no doubt, even though the recent discoveries of archæologists on various independent points of the ancient world did not all lead to the same conclusion. The researches of Dr. M. Ohnefalsch-Richter[1] in Cyprus, of Mr. Petrie[2] at Kahun and at Gurob, of Signor Ossi[3] in Sicily, etc., all give us glimpses of an established intercourse of the civilized peoples of the Mediterranean among themselves and with the East, long antedating the events brought before us by the objects now under consideration.

The fact that their relations with one another were sufficiently close to lead to an organized and concerted movement against so formidable a power as that of Egypt under the Ramessids—by such distant allies as the Libyans, the Maxyes, the Tyrrhenians, the Sikels, the Sardinians, the Achæans, and the Lykians in the second millennium B. C., as appears from the inscription of Karnak,[4] necessarily implies the existence of a long period, during which inter-commercial and political alliances could gradually be formed and cemented by the civilized Mediterranean nations of pre-Homeric times.

The recent discoveries of Mr. Petrie in the Fayûm, which tend to show that such a condition actually did exist in the ancient world at a much earlier period than has hitherto been admitted, interesting as they are, should logically have excited less surprise. The new facts

---

[1] See *Mittheil. der Anthrop. Gesells. in Wien*, November and December, 1890, and *Verhandl. Berlin. Anthrop. Gesells.*, January, 1891.

[2] *Kahun, Gurob, and Hawara*, 1890. The earliest mention of an Egyptian king making an expedition towards the people of the North—*i. e.*, the Ha henu—dates from the reign of S'Ankhara XI dynasty.

Mr. Petrie has found in the Fayûm traces of light-haired and other foreigners, and has gathered evidence to show that Etruskans, Libyans, and people of the Ægean Sea lived in the Fayûm as early as the third millennium B. C. In tombs of the XIIth dynasty he has found Cypriote pottery and vases similar to the earliest Italian pottery. Similar ware was also found by Mr. Naville at Kha'aneh, associated with objects of the XIIth and XIIIth dynasties. (See *Illahun Kahun Gurob*, p. 10.)

[3] Signor Ossi's researches in Sicily, conducted under governmental auspices, have shown that the Mykenæ culture extended as far as that island. The Siculi were probably among the people whom the hieroglyphic inscriptions above referred to describe as having taken part in the attack upon Egypt under Meneptah.

[4] Duemichen *Hist. Inscr.*, pl. ii. E. De Rougé *Les Attaques*, etc., pp. 8, 9.

fit in perfectly with the scientific probabilities of the question, as it now stands under the light shed upon it by other independent researches.

That such an intercourse, carried on, directly or indirectly, by the civilized Aryans with Egypt and Mesopotamia should have brought about an exchange of thought, and should have been the means of spreading certain arts and industries as far and as fast as the products of these could travel, requires no argument.

This fusion culminated, in the VIIth century B. C., with the foundation, in the Delta, of the Greek colonies of Daphnæ and Naukratis ; and we scarcely need wonder if, from the shores of Sardinia to the mountain fastnesses of Phrygia,[1] from Nubia to Würtemberg, we may even now, after millenniums, recover vestiges, faint though they at times may be, of the deep impression left upon the Aryan mind by ancient Oriental thought.

A cordial vote of thanks was offered Mrs. Stevenson for her address. A collection of Egyptian objects from the University Museum, comprising coins, bronze objects, and pottery was afterward exhibited. Mr. Culin exhibited a set of circular Indian playing cards from Lucknow, India.

MAY 7TH.

Mr. Culin read the following paper, entitled

"SYRIAN GAMES WITH KNUCKLE BONES."

At the beginning of a series of objects in the University Museum, designed to show the origin and development of the playing card, are a pair of small bones, which are familiarly known to English-speaking people as "knuckle bones." Seldom, if ever, used in this country, these bones, from the hind legs of sheep and certain other animals, have been famous for their employment in games from the time of classical antiquity. They are, in fact, the *astragali* of Greek and Latin authors. The four positions in which it is possible for them to fall were called by the latter *supinum*, *pronum*, *planum*, and *tortuosum*, and corresponded with the throws of three, five, one, and six with

---

[1] In the ornamentation of the facade of some of the rock-cut tombs of Phrygia, the lotus-bud, mixed with the Mesopotamian "palmette," in the well-known pattern so popular during the last millennium B. C., appears, along with the geometrical designs proper to the Thrakian style of decoration. Messrs. Perrot and Chipiez (*Hist. de l'Art*, v, p. 191) see in the peculiar execution of the lotus-bud above mentioned, an intention on the part of the artist to represent an acorn. But there is no possible doubt that the model, though perhaps misunderstood by the local artist, who was probably unacquainted with the form before him, was the common mixed lotus and palmette design so familiar to us.

dice. Certain dice—if not, indeed, the cubical dice—with which we are familiar, derived their origin from these natural objects, which were reproduced by the ancients in ivory, glass, and earthenware, in bronze, as seen in a fine example in Mr. Sommerville's collection in the Metropolitan Museum, New York, and even in precious metals, as gold itself. English boys used them in their games 200 years ago, according to that celebrated chronicler of games, Dr. Robert Hyde, and knew the four positions as "put in," "blank," "half," and "take all," a nomenclature that survives on a kind of tetotum, and may exist among English children at the present day. Among the Germans they are called *bückelbein*, and in France they are popularly used by the children as "jackstones," under the name of *osselets*, or "little bones."

Among the Turks, Arabs, Persians, and Armenians the four positions of the knuckle bones receive the names of as many classes of human society; thus, among the Persians, according to Dr. Hyde, they are called *Duzd*, "thief;" *Dihban*, "peasant;" *Vezir* and *Sháh*. It does not seem difficult to trace a connection between the throws thus designated and the coat cards of our playing cards, or even with the pieces in the game of chess, since chess is regarded by some to have been played originally according to the throws with dice.

Indeed, it may be assumed that these natural *astragali*, or "knuckle bones," occupy a most important place in the early development of many celebrated games. In view of this, and the fact that the recorded information concerning their use, especially in modern times, is not very satisfactory, it was with considerable pleasure that the writer was able to take down from the lips of a young Syrian, at present living in Philadelphia, the following account of games with knuckle bones as played by him in his childhood in his native city of Damascus:

It should be premised that the Arabic word *ka'b* (our word cube), by which these bones are called in Syria, as well as in many parts of the East, has the same meaning (the ankle, or the ankle bone), as their Latin name, *talus*, and the Greek, *astragalus*.

One of the commonest games among the Syrian boys is called *khut*. A circle of one, two or three yards in diameter is drawn on the ground, and the children each put in from one to five *ka'b*, which they range in a line across the middle of the ring. Then, standing opposite to this line, and toeing the circle, they each toss a *ka'b* at the row, and the one who comes nearest is entitled to play first. The game consists in knocking the *ka'b* out of the ring with another *ka'b*, which is held between the thumb and forefinger and thrown

as hard as possible, with a kind of twist. The *ka'b* from the right
and left leg constitute a pair, called respectively *yisr*, "left," and
yemene, "right," which are held somewhat differently in shooting.
The players shoot in turn, and each continues playing until he
fails to knock a *ka'b* out of the ring. After the first round they may
take any position they choose, always, however, toeing the circle.
The game continues until the last *ka'b* is knocked out, and is
played for "keeps."

Boys take their *ka'b* to school as our boys do marbles, and often
carry them in pockets made for the purpose in their voluminous
trousers, or in a bag which they suspend from their neck. They
buy them at butcher shops, where they are sold at the rate of from
two to five for one cent. The new ones are the most valued, as
they are stronger and heavier, and better in consequence to shoot
with. When a *ka'b* gets old, a hole is frequently bored in it and
filled with lead, in order to give it weight. It is important that the
shooter should be large and heavy. The sheep in Syria are larger
than the sheep of this country, and the *ka'b* are also larger. The
bones from cows and camels are sometimes employed, but they are too
large to be used by little children, and it is considered unfair to play
with them. The boys regard certain shooters as lucky, and value
them highly in consequence. "This one," they say, "will take three
at a throw." They call them by various names, such as "lion,"
"ostrich," "tiger," and a boy will often keep a favorite shooter for
a year or more. During recent years *ka'b* have fallen into disuse
among boys in cities like Damascus, having been supplanted by marbles, but they are still played by the country children.

Killet wa-ka'b, "marbles and *ka'b*," is also a popular game. The
players each put down the same number of *ka'b*, standing them on
their side, at a distance of one to two yards apart, along a straight line
at right angles to the base. They stand at the base and shoot in turn
with the marbles at the line of *ka'b* and endeavor to knock them over,
each taking the ones he overturns. If a player can hit another marble, the latter becomes *mat*, "dead" (the same word, mate, that we
use in chess), and must give up all the *ka'b* he has taken to the one
who hit him. The players shoot with their thumbs, as is the custom
here, or else rest their left hand on a support, as a piece of broken pottery, and drive the marble from it by forcibly twitching it with the
first or second finger of their right hand.

Kish stch is a game of tossing *ka'b*. In it the position called by
the ancients *planum* is called *kish*, while that called *tortuosum* is known

as *stich*. *Supinum* and *pronum* are known respectively as *qât*, "robber," and *chammâr*, "ass." Each player puts the same number of *ka'b* into the game, and the first player tosses them into the air. If one or more of them falls *kish* he takes all that at the same time fall *stich*. If one or more of them fall *qât*, "robber," he loses his turn, and if he has won any *ka'b* he must put back as many as fell *stich* into the game; or, if one or more fall *qât* and one or more *stich*, the throw is called *shisht*, and he must put back all he has won.

Ya Nasib is a kind of childish fortune-telling that recalls the " rich man, poor man, beggar man, thief," counted on the buttons of the coat among children here, and is a favorite amusement at children's entertainments. In it the four positions of the *ka'b*, are called *Sultan Vezir*, *Ashik*, "lover," and *Chammâr*, "donkey." The game is commenced by asking: " O, *ka'b*, what is so and so ?" mentioning the person by name. One *ka'b* is then thrown, and as it falls that person is declared to be a Sultan, Vezir, lover or donkey. Questions are then asked, such as, Where does he sit ? Where does he sleep ? With whom does he eat ? With whom does he talk ? and so on, which are answered : " With the Sultan," " With the Vezir," etc., according to the throws. The questions are concluded by asking : " O, *ka'b*, what will he become at last ?" This game is played by boys and girls, and by grown persons as well.

Matslûm is a game of forfeits. A number of players sit in a circle and throw one *ka'b* in turn. The one who first makes the throw of *kish* becomes Sultan, and the one who next throws either *kish* or *stich* Vezir. The latter twists his handkerchief or arms himself with a ruler to administer punishment. The other players then continue to throw in turn, and if the *ka'b* falls on its side in the positions before described, as *qât* or *chammâr*, the thrower cries out *anâ matslûm*—" I am aggrieved." The Vezir asks, " Who injured you ?" The player thereupon points out some one in the circle. The Sultan inquires of the injured one, " What shall we do with him ?" and the injured one tells the number of blows the Vezir shall inflict. Sometimes, instead of being beaten, the person who is accused is required to pay a forfeit. as by being made to dance or bark as a dog, kiss the hands of all present, or tell a story.

The Rev. Héli Chatelain, for some time a missionary at Loanda, Africa, presented through Mr. Culin a collection of bronze coins made for the colony of Angola by the Portuguese Government. A vote of thanks was offered to Messrs. Chatelain and Culin for the gift.

A photograph of the Count de Waldeck, bearing his autograph written in his 103d year, with a presentation copy of his memoir on *Le Sacrifice Gladiatorial* was presented by Francis C. Macauley, Esq., through the Recording Secretary. These objects were regarded with interest, as the Count de Waldeck had been a Corresponding Member of the Society, and the friend and correspondent of its late President, the Hon. Eli Kirk Price.

OCTOBER 1ST.

Francis Jordan, Jr., made a communication with reference to explorations he had recently conducted on Peter's Island in the Schuylkill River, where aboriginal relics had been found. The thick undergrowth interfered with his examination of the interior of the island; but at one end, where the bank had been washed away by the river, he discovered arrow-heads and a large quantity of fragments of Indian pottery.

Mr. Culin exhibited flat plaster casts of a set of 32 gambling sticks used by the Haidah Indians of the Northwest Coast, made from the original sticks in the United States National Museum, Washington. They bear impressions of the characteristic designs with which such sticks are frequently ornamented, and are intended for the collection of games in the Museum of Archæology in the University of Pennsylvania.

General Gates P. Thruston, of Nashville, Tenn., a Corresponding Member of the Society, presented a copy of his recent book entitled *The Antiquities of Tennessee*. A vote of thanks to General Thruston was ordered, commending his work as a valuable and important contribution to American archæology.

NOVEMBER 5TH.

Mr. Culin read the following paper on

"TIP-CATS."

In a recent communication to the *Journal of American Folk-lore* [1] I described the familiar game of "cat," or "pussy," which is constantly played by the boys in our streets, and I there referred to the convincing proofs of its antiquity furnished by Mr. Flinders-Petrie. In his excavations at Kahun, in the Fayoom, Egypt (cir. 2500 B. C.), he dis-

[1] Vol. IV, p. 233.

covered a number of "tip-cats," one of which, loaned to me by Mrs. Cornelius Stevenson, curator of the Egyptian Section of the Museum of the University, I have the pleasure to exhibit to you. The material of this object appears to be red cedar, probably hardened by the absorption of lime salts.

I have inquired about the existence of the game we call "cat" in other countries, and am informed that in Hohshan, in the province of Kwantung, China, it is played by children.[1] The pointed object used there is similar to the one used here, and is called *t'ò tsz'*, or "little peach." It is struck with a stick, in the manner practised here. For all that I know to the contrary, the game may be played by Chinese children generally, and is not confined to Hohshan. In Japan, on the contrary, according to a detailed account, for which I am indebted to Mr. Motochica Tsuda, of Tokio, there is only one place in that country where the game is played, that being in the district near Kumamoto, a city in the southern island. The game is there called *in ten*, and is played with a small stick, called *ko*, "son," and another stick, called *oya*, "parent." The latter is usually a foot or a foot and a half long, and is used to strike the *ko*.

Two boys play, one against the other, or one boy may play two or more, or equal sides of two or more may be chosen. A small pit is dug, and the *ko* placed on the edge, so that its end projects. One boy then strikes the projecting end with the *oya*. His opponent throws it from where it falls toward the little hole, and the batter then measures the distance from the place it last fell into the hole. If the batter after knocking the *ko* makes but one strike at it in the air, this distance is measured with the *oya*. If he hits it twice while in the air, it is measured first with the *oya* and then with the *ko*, and so on, alternately; and, if he hits it four times, the distance is measured exclusively with the *ko*. Each measurement with the *oya* or *ko* counts a point to the batter's credit. If the *ko* falls a distance less than the length of the *oya* from the hole, the batter goes out, and his opponent takes his place, or if an opponent catches the *ko* while it is in the air, the batter, and those on his side, if he has partners, lose all they have already made, and one of the other side takes the *oya*. The number chosen for the score is usually 100, which constitutes "game."

---

[1] F. Porter Smith, M. D., in an article on "Games of Chinese Children" (*The Phœnix*, No. 15, Sept., 1871) says: "*Ta-pang* is a game of 'cat' quite as dangerous to the eyes of bystanders in Chinese streets as in those of small English towns." *Ta-pang*—"to knock the stick."

It is Mr. Tsuda's opinion that, since the game is found in no other part of the empire than Kumamoto, it is probably of Corean origin The place was the site of the castle of General Kato, who took an important part in the campaign against Corea, 300 years ago. He ravaged the country so that traditions of his career still remain there. Those who were only able to fight he killed. The weak and infirm he turned loose to starve, but the skillful artisans he sent prisoners to Japan, to Kumamoto. As a result, several of the Corean arts survive there, such as the manufacture of porcelain and the Corean *amé*, "vegetable honey." The game of *in ten* Mr. Tsuda regards as probably introduced by these involuntary Corean immigrants.

DECEMBER 3D.

President Brinton read a paper on the use of weights and scales among some American tribes. Singular as it seems, the sense of weight, or the attribute of ponderosity, was nowhere employed in North America to measure quantity. The nearest approach to it was by the load a man could carry; but this was nowhere in the area referred to reduced to a fixed amount, nor was any apparatus in the nature of a balance, or scales and weights, invented by the natives. The same is positively asserted of the partially civilized Chibchas of New Granada by the early writers.

It is therefore the more surprising that we find evidence, both archæological and linguistic, that the ancient nations of Peru, both the Aymaras, Kechuas, and probably the Yuncas of the coast, manufactured and employed scales and weights of considerable perfection, and constructed on the most correct principles. Several such had come to the knowledge of the speaker, which had been disinterred from ancient Peruvian graves. One is in the American department of the British Museum. The bar is about eight inches in length ; to its extremities cords are attached, by which small cups or platforms are suspended. Evidently it was confined to the weighing of very small objects, probably gold. Two other specimens are in the possession of Professor Crawford of the Williamson school, near Philadelphia, also from Peru.

Turning to the evidence of language, we find that the Kechua and Aymara languages have a word in common for the balance, *huarcu ;* from which are derived the terms *huarcuni aycani*, to measure by weight, and others. It is true that *huarcuni* means "to hang something ;" *runa huarcuna*, "the man hanger" (*i. e.*, the gallows), in

Fig. 41.

Spanish, *la horca;* which might create
the suspicion that *huarcu* is a native form
of the Spanish word. It does not seem
to have been so regarded by the early
lexicographers nor by Middendorf in his
lately published Kechua lexicon. Moreover, in Aymara we have another word,
hiscana, which means scales or balances.
and also *achupalla,* which means the
weight of the balance ; and further, of the
same people, Bertonio, the old lexicog-
rapher, informs us that certain stones were
kept by the natives for use as standard
weights.

The evidence, therefore, seems conclu-
sive that in Peru, so far as is known,
alone in America, the native race had
reached this important invention.

Mr. Francis Jordan, Jr., exhibited two
copper implements found near Betterton,
on the Eastern Shore of Maryland. They
were discovered by a negro in plough-
ing, and consisted of a copper hoe blade
of the usual size and shape, and a leaf-
shaped lance head about 12 inches in
length. The latter implement (Fig. 41)
was pronounced by President Brinton to
be one of the most remarkable copper
objects he had ever seen. In form it was
more of a European than American type,
and was characterized by a flange which
extended through its entire length, and
yet it appeared to be, without question.
a work of native industry. Its base was
marked with deep notches made for the
purpose of securing it to the haft, and
the lower portion of the implement retained its original polish. The point
and upper portion were corroded and
without temper, the apparent presence of
which in the lower half of the implement

was one of its most interesting features. Mr. Jordan also gave an account of the shell heaps he recently examined near Betterton, at Still Pond Creek. He stated they were among the largest north of Florida. One measured between 15 and 16 feet in height, although for the past 60 years its shells had been carted away and burned for lime. The shells were all oyster shells, and broken. The heap contained pottery and numerous hammer stones. Mr. Jordan found there a piece of pot stone, pierced with a hole as if for use as a sinker, which he presented to the Society. The President stated that the Nanticoke Indians formerly inhabited the Eastern Shore of Maryland, and lived there until 1798.

Mr. Thomas Hockley exhibited two antique Etruscan necklaces, one of gold, of great beauty, and the other a mortuary necklace, of terra cotta. The latter was of exquisite finish, and consisted of double clay masks suspended from a chain. Mr. Culin exhibited a magical print from Fuhchau, China, designed to ward off harm from the thunder god.

www.ingramcontent.com/pod-product-compliance
Lightning Source LLC
Chambersburg PA
CBHW030618270326
41927CB00007B/1226